Behind the
Geometrical
Method

It is a general observation that people write as they read. As a rule, careful writers are careful readers and *vice versa*. A careful writer wants to be read carefully. He cannot know what it means to be read carefully but by having done careful reading himself. Reading precedes writing. We read before we write. We learn to write by reading. A man learns to write well by reading well good books, by reading most carefully books which are most carefully written.

Leo Strauss, *Persecution and the Art of Writing*

THE JERUSALEM SPINOZA
LECTURES OF 1984

EDWIN CURLEY

Behind the Geometrical Method

A Reading of Spinoza's *Ethics*

Princeton University Press
Princeton, New Jersey

For Julie and Paul

CONTENTS

PREFACE

THIS BOOK represents a much revised version of three lectures I gave in Jerusalem at the Hebrew University in May 1984, as the first Jerusalem Spinoza Lectures. In composing the original lectures I had in mind a double audience. I knew that many who would be present at those lectures would have a thorough knowledge of Spinoza, the literature on Spinoza, and philosophy generally. But I believed that just as many, perhaps more, would not be professional Spinoza scholars, but people who had only a little background in philosophy and an unsatisfied curiosity about Spinoza. I wanted my lectures to be helpful to the latter without being boring for the former.

In revising for publication in book form I have tried to keep both audiences in mind. The main text of the book is meant to be intelligible to the beginner, who knows little of philosophy, who has struggled with the *Ethics* and been defeated by it, but who is prepared to try harder. So I have generally kept scholarly clutter out of the main text. For the most part acknowledgments of indebtedness to other scholars, or of differences of opinion with them, and references to other philosophers, or to Spinozistic works other than the *Ethics*, are confined to the notes and to this preface. The general reader can skip the notes, and I encourage him to do so by making them endnotes rather than footnotes. But the reading of the *Ethics* which I offer in these pages is very much my own reading. As such it needs a good deal of defense. I would hope that the argument of the main text would be persuasive to many on its own. But specialists will find that much of the argument is conducted in the notes. The text of the book is, inevitably, considerably longer than the text of the lectures.

I hope no one will misunderstand this claim to write for the general reader. Nothing I can conscientiously do will make Spinoza *easy*. Reading this book with profit will require a willingness to read it carefully, and to engage patiently in some difficult and abstract reflections. It will require the kind of careful reading the *Ethics* itself requires. It will also help to have some general acquaintance with the philosophies of Descartes and Hobbes, who did much to set the problems with which Spinoza tried to deal and whose names will occur frequently here (Descartes throughout, Hobbes mainly in the final chapter). I try, when I invoke these names, to explain as much of their philosophies as is necessary to understand the relevant parts of Spinoza, but my ideal "beginner" would have read at least the *Meditations*, the *Passions of the Soul*, and most of the first two parts of the *Leviathan*.

In giving these lectures their general title, I have borrowed a phrase from Wolfson, whose *Philosophy of Spinoza* played an important role in my own first serious introduction to Spinoza, and whose methodology, understood in a certain way, is my inspiration on this occasion. In a famous passage Wolfson wrote:

> If we could cut up all the philosophical literature available to [Spinoza] into slips of paper, toss them up into the air, and let them fall back to the ground, then out of these scattered slips of paper we could reconstruct his *Ethics*.[1]

Taken strictly, of course, this claim is absurd. If Spinoza's thought had been that derivative from the thought of his predecessors, it would be of no interest.

But Wolfson doesn't really mean what he seems to say here. By the time we turn the page, we find him acknowledging that since the *Ethics* before us is not the result of a syncretism of traditional philosophy but rather the result of criticism, and since this criticism, though implied, is not explicitly expressed, we shall have to supply it ourselves.

And this is clearly a much more promising approach. You cannot explain what a philosopher means in saying something, or why he says it, merely by pointing out that some previous philosopher said the same thing, or something that sounds like the same thing. But if you can show how one philosopher's views might have arisen out of another's by forceful criticism of an inherently plausible position, then you can hope to write useful history of philosophy.[2]

Wolfson is right to assume that Spinoza's axiomatic style of presentation does not in fact provide the clarity Spinoza intended. The definitions are typically obscure, the axioms frequently not evident, and the demonstrations all too often unconvincing. And yet it is hard to escape the feeling that there is something there worth taking pains to try to understand, something very important, if true, and something quite possibly true. To see what that something might be, it seems a reasonable strategy to try to penetrate beneath the surface of the *Ethics* and to uncover the dialogue Spinoza was conducting with his predecessors, a dialogue the geometric presentation served to conceal, and was, perhaps, partly designed to conceal.

If my general procedure has much in common with Wolfson's, the execution will be quite different. No doubt many previous thinkers influenced Spinoza, form part of the intellectual background we need to understand in order to understand him. But I believe we have much more to gain from considering Spinoza's relation to Descartes and Hobbes than from examining his relation to any other previous authors. We can go quite a long way in understanding Spinoza without attending to any other predecessors. What I try to do in this book is to show how Spinoza might have arrived at many of his most distinctive doctrines through critical reflection on the Cartesian and Hobbesian systems. Part of Wolfson's problem is that he spends too little time relating Spinoza to his immediate predecessors and too much time relating him to a scholastic philosophy with which Spinoza had little sympathy. To ward off misunderstanding, let me emphasize the qualifications attached to what I have just said. I do not contend that we need attend only to Descartes and Hobbes in order to understand Spinoza, just that there seems to be more to be gained there than anywhere else.

I frequently refer, in the notes, to Spinozistic works earlier than the *Ethics*, and particularly to the *Short Treatise*. Whatever we may think about the dating and order of Spinoza's early works,[3] it is clear that the *Short Treatise* is an immature work, in the sense that in it Spinoza often seems confused, and certainly had not yet arrived at many of the views characteristic of the *Ethics*.[4] But precisely for that reason it is a very valuable document, since it shows us at least one stage Spinoza went through in arriving at the views argued for in the *Ethics*.

Methodology apart, there is also a substantive interpretive theme to this work. In recent years there has been a good deal of talk about Spinoza's dualism. Jonathan Bennett's stimulating *Study of Spinoza's "Ethics"* lists dualism as one of five "aspects of Spinoza's thinking which lie deeper than any of his argued doctrines and are so influential in his thought as to deserve special attention" (p. 29). By dualism Bennett means, roughly, the view that "the properties things have can be split cleanly into two groups, mental and physical, with no property belonging at once to both groups; this being so understood as to rule out any defining of mental terms through physical ones."[5] It is also understood to rule out any causal interaction between mental events and physical ones. My thought that that apple looks ripe is not part of the causal explanation of my reaching out my hand to pick it from the tree. Nor are the reflection of light rays from the surface of the apple or their action on my retina part of the causal explanation of my having the thought that the apple looks ripe.

This denial of interaction is an extremely paradoxical view. There can be no doubt that in some sense Spinoza held it, but there's room for much doubt about what it means, why he held it, and what its role is in his thought. My conviction is that it plays entirely too large a role in Bennett's interpretation of Spinoza.[6] One of the things I hope to accomplish in this book is to demonstrate the truth of that conviction, not so much by directly confronting Bennett's reading of Spinoza, as by setting out an alternative reading which, within the limits imposed by the fact that mine is a shorter book, does better justice to the texts which are our data.

Some scholars go further than Bennett in their talk of Spinoza's dualism. Bennett's Spinoza does hold that there is only one substance and that mind and body are one and the same thing. Bennett will allow that these doctrines make it reasonable to describe Spinoza as a monist, and perhaps even as a kind of materialist.[7] So in one sense Spinoza is a monist, in another he is a dualist. But according to Alan Donagan, the apparently monistic doctrines of Spinoza are on a par with the apparently geocentric doctrines of Descartes. In the *Principles of Philosophy* Descartes holds, in prima facie opposition to Copernicus, that the earth does not move (III, 28-29). And yet, as Donagan observes,

> historians of astronomy do not set Descartes down as an anti-Copernican or a geocentrist. For while he did formally disavow the proposition that Galileo and realist Copernicans were condemned by the Holy Office for af-

firming, he accompanied that denial with affirmations of numerous uncondemned propositions that were equally obnoxious to geocentrists . . . At the same time, he reconciled his formal disavowal of Copernicanism with his numerous Copernican affirmations by a radical doctrine of the nature of motion which neither Copernicans nor anti-Copernicans had seriously considered in this connection.[8]

Donagan offers this as an illustration of the general principle that

the totality of what anybody believes is a fabric of logically interconnected items, in which the sense of one is affected by the senses of the others. The very same sentence, uttered by different persons, whose other beliefs are different, may express different beliefs.

Whatever we may think of the analogy between Spinoza's monism and Descartes' geocentrism,[9] the general principle about meaning seems a plausible one. To see the force of statements like "mind and body are one and the same thing, expressed in different ways," we need to look carefully at the context in which they are embedded. But I think a thorough application of Donagan's principle of meaning to Spinoza's *Ethics* will lead to conclusions very different from those Donagan draws. One of the things I want to argue in this work is that Spinoza is best regarded as a kind of materialist,[10] more metaphysically sophisticated Hobbes, anxious to incorporate into his philosophy Cartesian insights which Hobbes could not appreciate, but a materialist nonetheless.

In closing let me take this opportunity to publicly thank Professor Yirmiahu Yovel for the invitation to deliver the lectures which provided the basis for this book, and for his kindness to Ruth and me during our visit to Jerusalem. Not only did I consider the invitation a great honor, but I was also pleased to have the stimulus to do something I have been wanting to do for some time. In the twenty-five years I have been working on Spinoza, I have written a good deal about him. But up until now everything I have written has focussed rather narrowly on some particular aspect of the system and has been addressed to a specialist audience, which I presumed to be generally familiar with Spinoza's writings, with the literature on Spinoza, and with developments in contemporary philosophy. But since my return to the United States from Australia in 1977 I have had to face the problem of teaching Spinoza to undergraduate and graduate students and have felt the need to do a different kind of work on Spinoza. The invitation to give a series of three lectures on Spinoza, to an audience who would for the most part not be Spinoza specialists, seemed just the right sort of opportunity.

If the truth is to be told, I also welcomed the opportunity to have another try at persuading Spinoza scholars of the fundamental soundness of the interpretation of Spinoza's metaphysics offered in my first book on Spinoza.[11] Not everyone who read that book, it seems, was wholly persuaded by it. No doubt some of the fault was mine, for adopting a style of exposition bound to lead even intelligent and careful readers to talk about a "speculative reinterpretation," rather than a simple interpretation. So one of the things I have tried to do in this book is to present some of the central ideas in my earlier work in a way less apt to raise charges of anachronism. The core of that interpretation, it seemed to me, could be presented in a way which would not give rise to those charges. It's been some eighteen years since I wrote that book. I've spent much of the intervening time translating Spinoza and working on Descartes and Hobbes. I think I understand my subject much better now, and I hope to be able to mount a more persuasive argument. But I do not assume any familiarity with my earlier work, and I am not sure that I myself now believe *all* of it to be correct.[12]

I would also like to acknowledge my indebtedness to a number of people who have commented on the manuscript in one stage or another: most notably, Dan Garber, Margaret Wilson, Don Garrett, Stuart Hampshire, and Stefan Koch. Their comments were extremely helpful. But my greatest debt is to Jonathan Bennett, not only for his comments on the manuscript, but also for writing a book on Spinoza which I find constantly challenging. Though I often disagree with him, and believe him to be wrong about some very fundamental matters of interpretation, I think no one who takes seriously the project of understanding the *Ethics* can afford to ignore the hard questions he raises about the text.

Finally, I should like to express my gratitude to the Guggenheim Foundation and to the National Endowment for the Humanities for supporting me during a portion of the time when I was working on this manuscript.

BIBLIOGRAPHICAL NOTE

THOUGH I try not to assume that readers will have much background in philosophy, I do assume that they will have a copy of the *Ethics* at hand, will have tried to understand it, and are prepared to try harder. Being human, I hope they have the translation contained in my edition of Spinoza's works (*The Collected Works of Spinoza*, vol. I, Princeton: Princeton UP, 1985), but I generally adopt a way of referring to Spinoza's text which will work no matter what edition they use. Most passages can be identified quickly enough using the following system of abbreviations:

E = the *Ethics*
KV = the *Short Treatise*
TdIE = the *Treatise on the Emendation of the Intellect*
PP = *Descartes' "Principles of Philosophy"* (i.e., Spinoza's attempt to put Descartes' *Principles* in geometric form)
CM = the *Metaphysical Thoughts*
Ep = Spinoza's correspondence
OP = Opera posthuma
NS = Nagelate Schriften (the Dutch translation of the OP, which also appeared in 1677)
I, II, III, etc., refer to parts of the work cited
A = axiom
P = proposition
D (following a roman numeral) = definition
1, 2, 3, etc., refer to axioms, definitions, propositions, etc.
D (following P + an arabic numeral) = the demonstration of the proposition

c = corollary
s = scholium
Post = postulate
L = lemma
Exp = explanation
Pref = Preface
App = Appendix
DefAff = the definitions of the affects at the end of Part III

So "E ID1" refers to the first definition of Part I, "E IIIP15C" to the corollary to proposition 15 of Part III, etc. Where that form of reference will not quickly locate the passage cited, I generally add volume, page and line numbers from the Gebhardt edition, which are given in the margins of my edition. For the TdIE and the KV, I make use of the section numbers given in my edition of the works.

For years we have not had a really satisfactory edition of Descartes' works in English, but now I think we can recommend *The Philosophical Writings of Descartes*, edited by John Cottingham, Robert Stoothoff and Dugald Murdoch (Cambridge: Cambridge UP, 1985, 2 vols.). This edition (CSM, for short) gives the Adam and Tannery pagination in the margins, and normally I shall simply use that pagination to make references to Descartes' works, whenever the passage in question is in CSM. The general reader should find CSM sufficient for most purposes. When I need to refer to a passage not in CSM, as I sometimes do, I use Kenny's edition of the correspondence (Descartes, *Philosophical Letters*, Minneapolis: U of Minnesota Press, 1981, abbreviated as K), the Millers' edition of the *Principles of Philosophy* (Dordrecht: D. Reidel, 1983, abbreviated as MM), and Cottingham's edition of the *Conversation with Burman* (Oxford: Clarendon Press, 1976, abbreviated as c). But passages in the *Principles* are generally identified most readily by part and section numbers. Similarly, I normally refer to the *Passions of the Soul* (abbreviated PA) by section numbers.

The study of Hobbes is handicapped by the fact that as of this writing there is no satisfactory standard edition of his works. For generations scholars have relied on the 19th edition by Molesworth, but that is now being replaced by the Clarendon edition under the editorship of Howard Warrender. So far only two volumes of the latter (the Latin and English versions of *De Cive*) have appeared. Fortunately it is generally possible to make a reference which will be independent of the particular edition used by citing chapter and section numbers (for *De Cive* and *De Homine*, abbreviated DC and DH, respectively), or part, chapter and section numbers (for the *Elements of Law*, abbreviated EL). The *Leviathan* (abbreviated *Lev*) presents a problem, since the chapters are not divided into numbered sections. I have used as section numbers the paragraph numbers of the MacPherson edition (Penguin, 1968), which is probably the most satisfactory edition for students. Students will find the relevant portions of DH and all of DC translated in *Man and Citizen*, ed. by Bernard Gert, Humanities / Harvester, 1978. For EL I use the edition by F. Tönnies, Frank Cass, 1969.

It is unclear, both in the case of Descartes and in the case of Hobbes, how much of their work Spinoza knew. For Descartes I assume that Spinoza was familiar with everything which had been published by, say, 1670, which would include everything which seems most important (e.g., the *Meditations*, the *Principles*, the *Passions of the Soul*, and the letters included in Clerselier's edition of the correspondence. I think it highly likely that Spinoza also knew the *Regulae* in a ms. version (Glazemaker, who translated much of Spinoza's own work into Dutch, published a Dutch translation of the *Regulae* in 1684, so we know that a ms. was circulating in the circle of Spinoza's friends). It seems less likely, but not impossible, that he also knew the *Conversation with Burman*. As for Hobbes, I assume that Spinoza knew everything which had been published in a language he could read by 1670. That would include, in addition to *De Cive, De Corpore, De Homine*, and the *Leviathan*, but not the *Elements of Law*.

Other works cited in shortened form are:

Allison = Henry Allison, *Benedict de Spinoza*, New Haven: Yale UP, 1986.

Alquié = F. Alquié (ed.), *Oeuvres philosophiques de Descartes*, Paris: Garnier, 1963-1973, 3 vols.

AT = Charles Adam et Paul Tannery, *Oeuvres de Descartes*, Paris: C.N.R.S. / Vrin, 1974-1986.

Bennett = Jonathan Bennett, *A Study of Spinoza's "Ethics,"* Hackett, 1984.

Beyssade = Jean-Marie Beyssade (ed.), *L'entretien avec Burman*, Paris: PUF, 1981.

Curley (1) = E. M. Curley, *Spinoza's Metaphysics*, Cambridge: Harvard UP, 1969.

Curley (2) = *Descartes Against the Skeptics*, Cambridge: Harvard UP, 1978.

Delahunty = R. J. Delahunty, *Spinoza*, London: Routledge & Kegan Paul, 1985.

Deleuze = Gilles Deleuze, *Spinoza et le problème de l'expression*, Paris: Minuit, 1968.

Donagan = Alan Donagan, "Spinoza's Dualism," in Kennington.

Grene = Marjorie Grene (ed.), *Spinoza, a collection of critical essays*, Anchor, 1973.

Gueroult = Martial Gueroult, *Spinoza*, Paris: Aubier-Montaigne, 2 vols., 1969, 1974.

Hampshire = Stuart Hampshire, *Spinoza*, New York: Penguin, 1951.

Kaufmann = Walter Kaufmann (ed. & tr.), *The Portable Nietzsche*, New York: Viking, 1964.

Kavka = Gregory Kavka, *Hobbesian Moral and Political Theory*, Princeton: Princeton UP, 1986.

Kennington = Richard Kennington (ed.), *The Philosophy of Baruch Spinoza*, Washington: Catholic University of America Press, 1980.

Lachièze-Rey = P. Lachièze-Rey, *Les origines cartésiennes du Dieu de Spinoza*, Paris: Vrin, 1950.

Mandelbaum and Freeman = Maurice Mandelbaum and Eugene Freeman, *Spinoza: essays in interpretation*, Open Court, 1975

Matheron = Alexandre Matheron, *Individu et communauté chez Spinoza*, Minuit, 1969.

Matson = Wallace Matson, "Death and Destruction in Spinoza's *Ethics*," *Inquiry* 20(1978):403-417.

Moore = G. E. Moore, *Some Main Problems of Philosophy*, New York: Collier, 1962.

Rodis-Lewis = Descartes, *Les Passions de l'âme*, intr. et notes par G. Rodis-Lewis, Paris: Vrin, 1966.

Wolfson = H. A. Wolfson, *The Philosophy of Spinoza*, Meridian, 1961.

Behind the
Geometrical
Method

I

On God

I. METHOD

SPINOZA ENDS the *Ethics* with the observation that "all things excellent are as difficult as they are rare" (VP42S). His subject at that point is the path to salvation—that is, to true peace of mind—but his words apply with equal force to the work they conclude. The *Ethics* is one of the great achievements of the human mind, but its difficulty matches its excellence. My goal in this book is to communicate such understanding as I think I have attained, in some twenty-five years of study, to as wide an audience as possible. My method will be to start from the philosophy of Descartes and to see how far the central themes of the *Ethics* can be derived from critical reflection on the Cartesian system.

In part, this approach is a heuristic device. When Descartes published his *Meditations*, it was a revolutionary work. But in the three and a half centuries which have passed since then, its ideas have seeped sufficiently into the consciousness of modern man that they have come to be part of educated common sense, much as Aristotle's philosophy was when Descartes wrote.[1] So trying to derive Spinoza from Descartes is a way of trying to make the abstractions of Spinoza's philosophy seem intelligible and reasonable, a way of going from the relatively familiar and natural to the unfamiliar and, prima facie, implausible.

But partly I choose to approach Spinoza in this way because I think that to some extent the process of reasoning I shall outline represents the way Spinoza himself arrived at those conclusions. Just how far my story tells his story I do not know. I don't mean to suggest that Spinoza was ever, at any point in his development, an orthodox Cartesian. It seems likely, in fact, that he had arrived at some of his most fundamental beliefs, beliefs he did not share with Descartes, before he had seriously encountered Descartes. But in the earliest substantial written works we have from Spinoza,[2] works written, probably, when he was in his late twenties, he appears to be thoroughly familiar with the Cartesian system and to have been, in some measure, influenced by it. His first published work, a careful exposition of Descartes' philosophy, which contains a good deal of (mainly implicit) criticism, was written while he was writing the *Ethics* and shows an interestingly ambivalent attitude. In the preface his friend Lodewijk Meyer wrote for that book, a preface Spinoza approved, Descartes is hailed as "the brightest star of our age," who has brought us "out of darkness and into light" (1 / 128 / 24-33). Nevertheless, Spinoza does not hesitate to have Meyer say on his behalf that he rejects many of Descartes' opinions as false. In the *Ethics* itself, Descartes has the distinction of being the only opponent mentioned by name, and twice at that. So it's clear that Spinoza gave a lot of thought to the Cartesian system, that he sympathized with much of it, as representing a promising revolution in philosophy, and yet that he believed Descartes had taken the wrong turn at various points on his way. This book will try to explore both the agreements and the disagreements and to show how some of the most distinctive features of Spinoza's philosophy arose from internal tensions within the Cartesian system.

2. THE IDEAL OF A UNIFIED SCIENCE

Let us begin with a point on which both Descartes and Spinoza agreed: that it is necessary, in a properly constructed philosophy, to proceed systematically, from metaphysical first principles, through an account of man and his place in nature, to a theory of the good for man. In Descartes this demand for a system of philosophy is most famously expressed in the letter to Picot which prefaces the French edition of the *Principles*:

> the first part [of true philosophy] is metaphysics, which contains the principles of knowledge, among which is the explanation of the principal attributes of God, of the immateriality of our souls, and of all the clear and simple notions which are in us. The second is physics, in which, after having found the true principles of material things, one examines in general how the whole universe is composed, then, in particular, what is the nature of this earth and of all the bodies most commonly found around it, like air, water, fire, magnets and the other minerals. Following this it is necessary also to examine in particular the nature of plants, of animals, and especially of man, so as to be able to find subsequently the other sciences which are useful to him. Thus the whole of philosophy is like a tree, whose roots are metaphysics, whose trunk is physics, and whose branches are all the other sciences, which reduce to three principal sciences: medicine, mechanics, and morals—I mean the most perfect morals, which, insofar as it presupposes a complete knowledge of the other sciences, is the highest degree of wisdom. (AT IXB, 14)

Spinoza will not agree with all of this. For example, he disagrees with Descartes about the order in which the various sciences are to be derived from metaphysics. He does not, as Descartes does, think that knowledge of the self must come before knowledge of God and of the material world. For Spinoza we must have knowledge of God before we have knowledge of the finite world, and we must have at least a rudimentary understanding of physics before we can work out a satisfactory theory of the human soul. That is the point of the excursus on the nature of bodies which occurs in Part II after PI3. But the general notion that philosophy, which here is not distinguished from human knowledge in general, can and should be organized into a deductive system which begins with metaphysics and ends in moral philosophy, after having considered the nature of man—that is an idea common to both Descartes and Spinoza, an idea which determines the structure of the works they wrote. Call it the ideal of the unity of science.[3]

3. CARTESIAN METAPHYSICS

So our investigation of the relation between their two philosophies must begin with metaphysics, where metaphysics is understood to be an attempt to

> give a general description of the *whole* of the Universe, mentioning all the most important kinds of things which we *know* to be in it, considering how far it is likely that there are in it important kinds of things which we do not absolutely know to be in it, and also considering the most important ways in which these various kinds of things are related to one another.[4]

If we were to give such a general description of the world as Descartes conceived it, it would be most natural to begin by saying that the world contains a great many substances, which are divided into two main kinds. On the one hand, there are material substances, like my body, and yours. On the other, there are immaterial substances, like my mind, and yours, and the divine mind, God. Most of these substances are finite. My body has certain dimensions, occupies a particular portion of space, but is limited in its extent. My mind is similarly limited insofar as there are thoughts it does not have, ideas it does not understand, things it desires but does not have. Only the divine mind is infinite, subject to no limitations or defects.

What Descartes implies, in calling these things substances, is that they all have some measure of independent existence. No doubt my body depends causally on a great many things for its continued existence. It would not remain in existence for long if it were not sustained by food and drink and air; and Descartes believes that it would not remain in existence for one moment if it were not sustained by God, who must continuously recreate it from one moment to the next. But it does not depend logically on any of these things. That is, we can conceive of its existing without any of these other things existing. Similarly with my mind. Each finite substance—i.e., each particular body, and each mind other than God—in virtue of its relative independence, is capable of existing without the others. So it is at least logically possible for my mind to exist without my body, and for my body to exist without my mind.

But not everything is thus independent. My body has a certain size and shape. We cannot conceive of a size or a shape without conceiving of it as the size or shape of some body. Similarly, my mind contains certain thoughts, which cannot be conceived except as the thoughts of some mind. There cannot be a thought—a desire or a belief, say—without there being a mind that thinks that thought. These dependent entities—sizes and shapes and thoughts—Descartes calls modes of the substances they depend on. As we have two kinds of substances, material and immaterial, so we have two kinds of modes, modes of material substances and modes of immaterial ones.

It's an essential feature of bodies that they are extended in three dimensions, but not an essential feature of them that they have the particular size and shape they have. My body will not cease to be my body, even though its size and shape change,[5] but it would cease to be my body, would cease to be *a* body, would cease to exist at all, if it ceased to be extended.

Similarly, it is not essential to my mind that it have the particular thoughts it has, but it is essential to it that it have some thoughts or other. If it ceased to think, it would cease to be. So Descartes gives a special status to thought and extension. Thought he calls the principal attribute of mind, because it is the most fundamental property of minds, their essential property, of which all their more transient properties are particular specifications. Extension he calls the principal attribute of body, because it is the most fundamental property of bodies.

In its general outlines, if not in all its detail, this Cartesian picture of the world as consisting of a great many substances, which fall into these two principal kinds, is a very commonsensical picture. If there is any such thing as a common-sense view of the world, I think it must be pluralistic as regards the number of substances there are, and dualistic as regards the kinds of substance there are, though common sense might not now choose to express its view in the language of substances, attributes and modes, and might not have any very definite view about what constitutes the essence of bodies or of minds, or about how the divine mind differs from finite minds.[6] That is one reason why it is interesting to juxtapose Spinoza and Descartes. If we can show that the Cartesian metaphysic leads by plausible steps to the Spinozistic one, then we will have shown that a very natural way of looking at the world contains within it the seeds of Spinozism.

4. SPINOZISTIC METAPHYSICS

The most striking and obvious difference between Spinoza's metaphysics and Descartes' is that Spinoza denies Descartes' pluralism about substances, denies that there are many distinct substances. For him there is only one substance, the infinite substance, God (E I P14); all the particular things Descartes regarded as finite substances Spinoza says are modes which express the attributes of God in a certain way (IP25C).

There are many other differences, of course, but this one is central, and I want to begin by trying to understand it. In spite of Spinoza's conscientious efforts to explain what he means by his technical terms and to set out a step-by-step argument for each of his propositions, and in spite of three hundred years of commentary by some very good minds, it is still not clear what Spinoza means by this thesis, or why he thinks himself entitled to affirm it. I propose to begin by tackling the question of his entitlement to the thesis first, and only then to ask what it all means, in the expectation that a careful look at the process of derivation will shed light on the question of meaning.

5. THE ARGUMENT FOR P14

Suppose we look at the chain of argument leading up to IP14, which says:

Except God, no substance can be or be conceived,

and ask ourselves at what point of that argument Descartes might have objected to the proceedings. P14 is derived from the definition of God, D6:

By God I understand a being absolutely infinite, i.e., a substance consisting of an infinity of attributes, of which each one expresses an eternal and infinite essence;

from P11:

God, or a substance consisting of infinite attributes, each of which expresses eternal and infinite essence, necessarily exists;

and from P5:

In nature there cannot be two or more substances having the same nature or attribute.

9

The idea behind the demonstration of P14 is beautifully simple: if there must be a substance which has infinite attributes (where having infinite attributes implies having *all possible* attributes), and if there can't be two substances which have the same attribute, then the existence of the substance with infinite attributes (God) excludes the possibility of there being any other substance.

Suppose we agree, for the time being, that Descartes would accept Spinoza's definition of God. It's not immediately evident that he would, but I think he would have difficulty rejecting it, and I want to postpone argument on that point until later (§9). If we assume Descartes would accept D6, we must also assume he would raise no objection to P11. He might not like the way Spinoza claims to prove P11,[7] but he could hardly reject the proposition itself, since he is committed by his version of the ontological argument to holding that God exists necessarily, in the sense that his essence involves existence, i.e., that, given the concept we have of God, it would involve a contradiction for us to suppose that he does not exist.

So if Descartes accepted P5, he would find it hard to reject the proof of P14. But clearly Descartes would not accept P5,[8] since he thinks there are a great many different substances sharing the attribute of thought, and since he holds (or usually seems to hold) that there are a great many different substances sharing the attribute of extension.[9] So the question becomes: how good is the argument for P5? on what grounds might Descartes object to its demonstration?

6. THE ARGUMENT FOR P5: THE OPENING

Let's begin by simply listing the ultimate assumptions on which P5 is supposed to rest. The proof itself cites a definition and an axiom that looks like a definition:

D3: By substance I understand what is in itself and is conceived through itself . . .

A6: A true idea must agree with its object.

It also cites P1, which is supposed to follow directly from the definition of substance, together with the definition of mode:

D5: By mode I understand the affections of substance . . .

and P4, which is supposed to follow from the definitions of substance and mode, together with the definition of attribute:

D4: By attribute I understand what the intellect perceives of substance, as constituting its essence;

and an axiom:

A1: Whatever is, is either in itself or in another.

Which of these assumptions might Descartes object to, and object to in a way which would affect the conclusions Spinoza wants to derive from them?

Not, I suggest, to the definition of substance, since he offers a very similar definition himself in the *Principles of Philosophy*:

By substance we can understand nothing other than a thing which so exists that it needs no other thing in order to exist. (I, 51)

No doubt there are differences between this definition and Spinoza's, but I do not think there are any which are crucial to P5D and I think we can take Descartes' definition as providing us with a gloss on the notion of "existing in itself."[10]

Nor do I think Descartes would object in any material way to the definition of attribute, since, again, he offers a similar account himself:

Each substance has one principal property, which constitutes its nature and essence and to which all its other
properties are referred. (*Principles* I, 53)

Again, there may be differences between Spinoza's formula
and Descartes', but none which seem to affect the argument.[11]

Nor can we imagine Descartes' objecting to Spinoza's definition of mode (cf. *Principles* I, 56), to A1, or to A6. If there is
an objection, it must be to the way Spinoza derives P1, P4, or
P5 from these initial assumptions.

Now P1 seems harmless enough. It says simply that "Substance is prior in nature to its affections." Spinoza does not
explain what he means by "prior in nature" but we can make
a pretty good guess from the fact that he thinks it evident from
D3 and D5. If a substance is something which exists in itself in
the sense of needing nothing else in order to exist, and if a
mode is something which does need something else in order to
exist, the substance whose "affection" it is, then modes depend on substances for their existence, while substances do
not depend on modes for their existence. If that is what Spinoza means by saying that substances are prior in nature to
modes, it is just good Cartesian doctrine. Let's assume that is
what he means.

7. MIDDLE GAME: THE ARGUMENT FOR P4

The demonstration of P4 is less straightforward, but short and
important enough to be worth quoting in full:

P4: Two or more distinct things are distinguished from
one another, either by a difference in the attributes of the
substances or by a difference in their affections.

Dem.: Whatever is, is either in itself or in another (by
A1), i.e. (by D3 and D5), outside the intellect there is nothing except substances and their affections. Therefore,

there is nothing outside the intellect through which a
number of things can be distinguished except substances,
or what is the same (by D4), their attributes, and their
affections.

The first sentence of the demonstration is unproblematic,[12]
but the second one may well come as a surprise. For it treats
D4 as licensing an identification of a substance with its attribute. And this may seem both uncartesian and unspinozistic:
uncartesian, it will be said, because Descartes would surely
not confuse the attribute of extension with the extended thing
which has the attribute; unspinozistic, because Spinoza holds
that there is only one substance but infinitely many attributes.[13]

Identifying substance and attribute *seems* uncartesian, but
is it? I think not. Certainly there are Cartesian texts which
make a distinction between substance and attribute,[14] but his
official position is that the distinction is only a distinction of
reason, and his explanation of that position shows a strong
tendency to identify the substance with its principal attribute:

There is a distinction of reason between a substance and
an attribute of substance without which the substance itself cannot be understood . . . This is recognised from the
fact that we cannot form a clear and distinct idea of that
substance if we exclude that attribute from it . . .

Thought and extension can be considered as constituting the natures of thinking and corporeal substance; and
then they must not be conceived otherwise than as thinking substance itself and extended substance itself, i.e., as
mind and body . . . we understand extended substance or
thinking substance more easily than we understand substance alone, i.e., than when we omit the fact that it is
thinking or is extended. For there is some difficulty in ab-
stracting the notion of substance from the notions of

thought and extension, which differ from substance only by reason . . .

Thought and extension can also be taken as modes of substance, insofar as one and the same mind can have many different thoughts, and insofar as one and the same body, though retaining the same quantity, can be extended in many different ways . . . then [thought and extension] are distinguished modally from substance . . . (*Principles* I, 62-64)

Making a modal distinction between a mode of thought, say, and the thinking thing whose mode it is, implies that the thinking thing can be understood without the mode, but not conversely, i.e., the mode cannot be understood without the substance (I, 61). But making a distinction of reason between thought, considered as an attribute, and the substance which has that attribute, implies that the substance cannot be understood without the attribute.

I take it that Descartes' view here is this: at a certain level of generality we can make a distinction between a thing, or substance, and its properties; when I ascribe a mode to an extended thing—say that the table is three feet long—there is some content to the distinction between the mode and the thing whose mode it is, because we can have some conception of what the thing (the table) would be without that property (extended, rectangular, four feet long, perhaps); but when the property in question is as fundamental a property as an attribute, we cannot conceive of what the thing would be like without that property; to try to suppose a world in which the table had become a mind, a thinking, non-extended substance, would be to try to suppose something unintelligible—how would that supposition differ from supposing that the table had ceased to exist and been replaced by a mind?—so at that level of generality we must conceive of the thing as having that property if we are to conceive of it at all; the attempt to conceive of a substance without its principal attribute is empty.[15]

If the notion of a substance in abstraction from the attribute which constitutes its essence is empty, then that notion cannot be used to distinguish two things from one another. It is not just that *we* cannot have a clear idea of a substance in abstraction from its principal attribute. We do not mean to state a limitation of the human intellect, which other, higher intellects might not be liable to. Rather we are saying something about the intrinsic nature of that concept. So P4 does not mean merely that *we* cannot distinguish things by anything other than their attributes and their modes. No intellect could.[16]

8. THE ARGUMENT FOR P5: ENDGAME

Let us turn now to P5: "In nature there cannot be two or more substances of the same nature or attribute." The demonstration begins easily enough, by citing the proposition just demonstrated, P4. The argument then proceeds:

> If [two distinct substances were distinguished] only by a difference in their attributes, then it will be conceded that there is only one of the same attribute.

That is, since, by hypothesis, we are discussing substances which have the same attribute, we cannot use their attribute to distinguish them. And that may well seem reasonable enough.

Nevertheless, this step is not without its problems. Long ago Leibniz asked: why can't there be two substances, one having attributes A and B, the other having attributes B and C? Then they will have the same attribute, B, yet be distinguished by the fact that one has attribute A, but lacks attribute C, whereas the other has attribute C, but lacks attribute A.[17]

We might be inclined to reply, on Spinoza's behalf, that when he paraphrases P5 in P8D, he does so in the following terms:

A substance *of one attribute* does not exist unless it is unique [i.e., the only one of its kind; my emphasis].

This suggests that Spinoza is interpreting P5 as limited to substances which have only one attribute.[18] But this reply may not seem sufficient to avoid the objection. After all, what Spinoza *needs*, for the argument of P14, is an unrestricted version of P5: "No two substances can have the same attribute, no matter how many attributes they have." Since he himself later insists that "it is far from absurd to attribute many attributes to one substance" (1P10S, II / 52 / 9), and since he believes in the existence of a substance, God, which has all possible attributes (P11), how can he proceed at this point on the Cartesian assumption that each substance has only one attribute?

Clearly Leibniz's objection to Spinoza is one Descartes himself could not make without giving up his contention that the attributes constitute the essences of the substances which we speak of as 'having' them. So Spinoza's argument seems effective at least against Descartes. But is it only an *argumentum ad hominem*? That will depend on how far the rest of us share Descartes' intuitions. I take it that there is a real problem involved in explaining how it is that a being with two attributes would constitute one being rather than two. If we can have no conception of substance apart from its principal attribute, what are we saying of a substance when we say that it is one, yet has two attributes? In the special case of God, there may be a solution to that problem (see below, §11). In the case of beings with some, but not all, attributes, I can see no such solution.

So I take it that Leibniz's criticism does not pose an insuperable difficulty, and I pass to the next (and last) step in the argument for P5:

> But if [they were distinguished] by a difference in their affections, then since a substance is prior in nature to its affections (by P1), if the affections are put to one side and [the substance] is considered in itself, i.e. (by D3 and A6), considered truly, one cannot be conceived to be distinguished from another, i.e. (by P4), there cannot be many, but only one [substance of the same nature or attribute].

The crucial questions here are what Spinoza means by putting the affections or modes "to one side" and why he should feel entitled to do that by the fact that the substance is prior to its affections. To answer these questions, let's try to put them in a Cartesian context by considering the implications of one of the most famous passages in the *Meditations*.

I mean that passage at the end of the Second Meditation (AT VII, 30) in which Descartes analyzes the piece of wax. We start with a piece of wax freshly drawn from the hive: it is sweet, hard, fragrant, and cold; it has a certain color, a certain size, a certain shape; if you strike it, it emits a certain sound. Now we take it close to the fire and all of these qualities, all of the modes of the wax, change: it loses its taste, its fragrance, changes its color and size and shape; it becomes liquid and hot; if you strike it, it no longer emits a sound. Does the same body still remain?[19] Yes, Descartes says, no one denies this, no one thinks otherwise. Why, then, do I judge that the same body remains? Because of the only thing that remains constant through all these changes: there is an extended something here, capable of change. This is an argument for the Cartesian doctrine that the essence of body consists in extension in three dimensions.

Now let us place beside the wax the stone used to make the same point in the *Principles*. What distinguishes it from the wax? Well, of course, it has different sensible qualities, different modes: it is harder than the wax was even before we brought the wax near the fire; its color is different; perhaps its size and shape are also different, and so on. It will not change these qualities as readily as the wax will change its qualities. But we cannot rest the distinction between the wax and the stone on these modes since the analyses of the wax and the stone show that these modes are merely accidental to these things. All the modes of either body might change while the same bodies still remained. If so, there is no reason in principle why the stone might not come to have precisely the same modes as the wax. But if these two bodies might have precisely the same modes, and remain two distinct bodies, the distinction between them cannot be based on their modes.[20]

Common sense might want to say that the wax and the stone are distinguished from one another because each occupies a different location in space. But this will not be an admissible answer in the Cartesian system. According to Descartes, the distinction between a body and the space it occupies is not a real one. The same extension which constitutes the nature of body constitutes the nature of the space it is said to occupy.[21]

If a distinction between two bodies cannot be based on their modes, because the modes are too peripheral, or on their attributes, because they have the same attribute, and if two extended substances, to be *two* distinct substances, must be distinguishable either by their modes or their attributes, then we cannot conceive of two substances which share the attribute of extension. If there is any extended substance at all, there is only one. And surely there is at least one extended substance. This line of reasoning may help to explain why Descartes sometimes suggests that there is only one extended substance, the whole of physical nature.[22]

I take it that the same dialectic applies with even greater force to minds.[23] One mind can't be distinguished from another by a difference in modes, because, the modes being accidental, inessential, all the modes of the first mind could be altered so that they were exactly the same as those of the second mind, without the first mind's thereby becoming a numerically different thinking thing. One mind can't be distinguished from another by a difference in attribute because they both have the same attribute, thought. One can't be distinguished from another by a difference in substance, because we have no conception at all of substance apart from the attribute which we speak of it as having. And in the case of minds, the question of their being distinguished by spatial location does not even arise, since minds, as such, have no spatial properties. But if there is nothing by which different minds might be distinguished from each other, they cannot be really distinct, in the sense that they are not substances, capable of existing apart from one another. But if they are not substances, they must be modes, and there must be a thinking substance whose modes they are. So we reach, apparently, the conclusion that there can be only one thinking substance, of which individual finite minds are complex modes, just as individual finite bodies are complex modes of one extended substance.

9. THE DEFINITION OF GOD

In the last three sections we have been exploring Spinoza's rationale for P5, the most obviously controversial step in Spinoza's proof that there is only one substance. The argument is complex and difficult enough that doubts may well remain about its soundness, but let's suppose it works. That leaves one more crucial link to be tested in the chain of argument leading to P14: the definition of God. Earlier I suggested Descartes might resist that definition, but would have difficulty in doing so. Let me now try to make good on that suggestion.

To understand the Spinozistic pressures operating on Descartes, we need to explore the way Descartes derives his philosophical conception of God, dialectically, from more popular conceptions of God, in the *Meditations*.[24] Descartes introduces the concept of God in the First Meditation as the concept of a being who possesses two attributes:[25] he is omnipotent and he is my creator. That I believe myself to have been created by an omnipotent being is a reason for doubting even the simplest truths of mathematics. If I was created by an omnipotent being, surely he could have created me in such a way that I might be deceived even about all those things that seem clearest of all to me. But no sooner does Descartes introduce this ground of doubt than he proceeds to doubt it. God is said to be extremely good, so perhaps he would not deceive, even though he can. Still, there can be no doubt that I am sometimes deceived. How is this possible, if I have been created by a supremely good God?

One way of looking at the argument of the *Meditations* is as a reflection on the divine attributes.[26] Perhaps the term "God" should be reserved for a being who combines all the attributes mentioned so far: omnipotence, supreme goodness, and being the creator of all things. Perhaps what we mean by the term "God" is just a being who has all those attributes. But our possibly arbitrary definition cannot legislate such a being into existence. We cannot solve the problem of the possibility of divine deception simply by listing the various attributes contained in our concept of God. For those attributes may not all be combined in one being. Perhaps there is no God in the sense in which we understand that notion. Perhaps the closest approximation in reality to God as we understand him is a being who has only some, not all, of the attributes contained in our concept of God. Perhaps our creator is a being who is omnipotent, but not supremely good. Not to violate the conventions of our language, we shall call him the "Evil Spirit," understanding by that term a being who combines the attributes of omnipotence, being the creator of all things other than himself, and being supremely malicious. Perhaps the Evil Spirit, not God, is my creator.

As I read the *Meditations*, Descartes' answer to this question is that, on reflection, we find the concept of the Evil Spirit to be incoherent. The attributes defining the Evil Spirit cannot be combined in one being, for the attributes involved in our concept of God are necessarily connected with one another. We discover this as follows. In the Third Meditation we ask whether God exists and can be a deceiver. Answering those questions requires an analysis of our idea of God. Initially the analysis proceeds as it had in the First Meditation, by an enumeration of God's attributes. But as the Third Meditation proceeds, Descartes gives various lists of the divine attributes. His first (AT VII, 40) adds attributes not mentioned in the First Meditation—eternity, infinitude, and omniscience—and omits the attribute which had previously been called in question—goodness. A later list (AT VII, 45) adds yet another attribute, independence, and again omits attributes previously mentioned, goodness and eternity.

These interesting variations suggest that the procedure of defining God by enumerating his attributes is inherently unsatisfactory. How do we know which attributes belong on our list and which do not? How do we know when we have specified enough attributes to have given a satisfactory analysis of our idea? How do we know that all of these attributes are compatible? How do we know the closest approximation in reality to God as we conceive him is not a being who has some, but not all, of these attributes?

Descartes achieves a decisive advance in his reflection on the divine attributes when, late in the Third Meditation, he defines God as a supremely perfect and infinite being (AT VII, 46).[27] This gives him a principle for determining which attributes belong on the list and which do not:

Whatever I clearly and distinctly perceive that is real and
true and implies some perfection, the whole of it is contained in this idea [of a supremely perfect being]. It does
not matter that I do not comprehend the infinite, or that
there are innumerable things in God which I cannot comprehend, and perhaps will not even be able to attain any
conception of. (AT VII, 46)

It does not matter that his analysis of the idea of God cannot
be exhaustive, because now at least he has a principle for deciding individual cases, a principle arrived at by generalization
from the various lists produced by his initial reflections, a
principle entailing the existence of other previously unsus-
pected attributes.[28]

How close we are getting to a Spinozistic definition of God
becomes even clearer when we look at the way Descartes defines the concept in the Geometric Exposition which follows
the Second Replies:

A substance which we understand to be supremely perfect, and in which we can conceive absolutely nothing
which involves any defect, or limitation of perfection, is
called *God*. (AT VII, 162)

If God is supremely perfect, we cannot conceive of him as
lacking any property which involves any perfection, and we
must conceive of him as possessing each such property in a
way which does not involve any limitation. That is, if God is
supremely perfect, he must be absolutely infinite in the sense
in which Spinoza understands that term (cf. E 1D6, Exp).
Given this understanding of what supreme perfection involves, it is not surprising that in one of his early letters Spinoza should infer his definition of God immediately from the
Cartesian one:

I define God as a being consisting of infinite attributes, each of which is infinite, or supremely perfect, in its kind ... That this is a true definition of God is clear from the fact that by God we understand a being supremely perfect and absolutely infinite. (Letter 2, IV / 7 / 24-8 / 3)

This definition will be carried over to the *Ethics* with only minor transformations. There the focus will be put on the notion of absolute infinity. But that notion will be explained in the same way Descartes explains the notion of supreme perfection. On the face of it, Descartes' definition of God and Spinoza's are equivalent.

10. WHAT COUNTS AS AN ATTRIBUTE?

Someone might object here that all this is too quick. Descartes and Spinoza may agree in their conception of God so long as we attend only to the most abstract formulas they use to define God, but when we ask ourselves what, in more concrete terms, those formulas come to, we find they differ radically. A Cartesian list of God's attributes will contain such items as: omnipotent, creator of all things other than himself, supremely good, omniscient, infinite, eternal, independent, etc. A Spinozistic list will contain such items as: thinking, extended, etc. There is no overlap between the two lists, and each list contains some items the other will absolutely deny to God. Spinoza does not think God is the *creator* of anything, since he thinks the very concept of creation is incoherent.[29] Descartes does not think God is extended, because he thinks being extended necessarily involves being divisible, and hence, imperfect, so that extension cannot be ascribed to a supremely perfect being. (*Principles* I, 23)

We touch here on a point to which Spinoza attached great

importance. In one of his early letters he wrote to Oldenburg to ask advice about publishing a treatise on which he was then working, a treatise which would explain "how things have begun to be and how they depend on the first cause" (Letter 6). He worried about offending the preachers, he said, because he regarded

> as creatures many "attributes" which they, and everyone, so far as I know, attribute to God. Conversely, other things, which they, because of their prejudices, regard as creatures, I contend are attributes, which they have misunderstood. (IV / 36 / 19-23)

The treatise he here refers to is almost certainly the *Short Treatise*,[30] where he complains about the philosophers who

> have defined God as a *being existing of himself, cause of all things, omniscient, omnipotent, eternal, simple, infinite, the greatest good, of infinite compassion*, etc. (KV I, vii, 2; I / 44 / 11)

None of these, he says, are properly regarded as attributes of God. Although they may belong to God in the sense that they are properly predicated of him, they do not explain *what* God is, i.e., they do not pertain to God's essence, as an attribute, in the strict sense of the term, should.

We can understand what is at stake here most easily by considering omniscience. Spinoza entertains no doubt that this is a property of God. But it is not a fundamental property of God, as an attribute strictly so-called is required to be: it presupposes the property of thought. An omniscient being must be a thinking being, though a thinking being need not be omniscient. So omniscience, along with other properties in the same vein (being wise, being compassionate), is only a mode of the thinking thing, rather than an attribute of substance (KV I, vii, 7; I / 45 / 21).

Analogously, God's omnipresence presupposes that he is an extended thing (κν I, vii, I n.a; I / 44 / 34). If we are to understand this property of God, we must first ascribe to him the more fundamental property of extension.[31] Other properties of God—e.g., that he is the cause of everything—are ascribed to God in virtue of all of his attributes. God is the cause of some things, e.g., modes of thought, in virtue of the fact that he is a thinking thing, and of others, e.g., modes of extension, in virtue of the fact that he is an extended thing (E IIP6). If God did not have both the attributes of thought and extension, he would not be able to cause either modes of thought or modes of extension, for if one thing has nothing in common with another, it cannot be its cause (IP3).

Now Descartes would presumably accept the point about omniscience. It is a curious feature of his various lists of divine attributes that they generally do not mention thought,[32] but surely he would agree that God is a thinking thing,[33] and it's hard to see how he could deny that this is a logically more fundamental property than omniscience.

But there is, Descartes would argue, a problem about extension. It's true that extension has "some perfection" in it (*Principles* I, 23), and that Descartes has so defined God that whatever has any perfection in it must be contained in the idea of God (see above, §9). It's true also Descartes would have some sympathy with the Spinozistic axioms which exclude the possibility of a thinking and non-extended substance's being the cause of an extended and non-thinking substance (cf. E IP3D). Cartesian causes are supposed to entail their effects. It is not supposed to be logically possible for the cause to exist and the effect not exist.[34] And it's hard to see how there can be relations of entailment between things which have no conceptual connection. How can one thing be deducible from another when the thing deduced has nothing in common with the thing from which it is deduced? But we can deal with the principles pushing us in a Spinozistic direction by simply qualifying them.[35] And we must do this, since it is evident that extension implies divisibility, which in turn implies imperfection.

Spinoza's reply is to deny that an extended substance must be divisible (E IP13C). It's a rather surprising reply, I think, but one which becomes more understandable the more we reflect on the nature of extended substance, as Descartes conceives it. We might begin by asking why divisibility is supposed to be an imperfection. The natural answer is that divisibility implies destructibility, and destructibility is self-evidently an imperfection. Something which is perfect will not be liable to destruction. Now P5 has shown that there can be at most one extended substance. And if we do not question our natural belief that there is at least one extended substance, we must accept that there is exactly one extended substance, which we may identify with the physical world as a whole. So now we ask: is this one extended substance divisible? If it is divisible, it must be divisible into parts. Then the question becomes: what is the character of the parts into which the extended substance is supposed to be divided? Specifically, are those parts *really distinct* from one another in the Cartesian sense of that term, i.e., are they substances, capable of existing apart from one another?

If P5 is right, they cannot be substances capable of existing apart from one another, since that would require there to be two substances sharing the same attribute. But we don't have to rely on P5 at this point. We can simply ask ourselves whether the parts of the one extended substance could exist apart from one another. Can one portion of extension cease to exist while the others remain? How could a portion of extension cease to exist? We might imagine the piece of wax suddenly vanishing, leaving behind only what we naively call "empty space." But in fact that space will likely be filled by air. And even if it is not, the wax will leave behind the same space, the same portion of extension. And that's all the wax really was, a portion of extension which was qualified in certain ways different from the portions of extension around it. So it would be more accurate to say that the wax has not disappeared, but rather that the portion of extension which it was has come to be differently qualified. One part of the extended substance cannot cease to exist while the others remain. I.e., the extended substance cannot be divisible in any sense which would imply destructibility.[36] So there is no reason to deny that extension is an attribute of God, and there are at least three good Cartesian reasons to affirm that it is: extension does contain some perfection, some degree of reality; we need to attribute extension to God in order to understand how he can be omnipresent; and we need to attribute extension to God to understand how he can be the cause of extended things.

II. SUBSTANCE AND ATTRIBUTE AGAIN

The preceding section dealt with one problem raised by my claim that Descartes' definition of God is equivalent to Spinoza's, that their verbal similarity masks substantive disagreements about the nature of God. If I am right, Descartes had not properly worked out the logic of his own position. Here's another problem. According to Descartes, each substance has one principal attribute which constitutes its nature or essence. For minds that attribute is thought; for bodies, extension. Descartes will allow that some other invariant properties of things—existence and duration, for example—may also be called attributes (*Principles* I, 56), but they are not *principal* attributes, constituting the nature of the things they belong to: they do not explain *what* the things are. If you knew about a thing only that it existed, or that it had duration, you would not know anything of substance about it, whereas if you knew that it was extended or thinking, you would know which of the two most general kinds of thing it belonged to and what kinds of modes it could be expected to have. For Descartes, each substance can have only one principal attribute.

For Spinoza, on the other hand, the one substance is supposed to "consist of" infinite attributes, each of which is what Descartes would call a principal attribute, in the sense that it constitutes the essence of the substance it belongs to. Or rather, since these attributes are supposed to be really distinct from each other, in that each can be conceived without the aid of the other (IP10S; II / 52 / I), perhaps we should say that each constitutes *an* essence of the one substance. But how can one thing have many essences?

When the question is put this way, Spinoza's answer, as given in IP10S, seems to be as follows: we are not entitled to assume that two distinct attributes *must* constitute two distinct substances, for we can conceive of a being which has more than one attribute, indeed, infinitely many attributes: God. The conception we have of God, as a supremely perfect being, forces us to ascribe to him whatever has any perfection in it. We know there are at least two attributes having some perfection in them, extension and thought, so we know those two attributes at least must belong to the supremely perfect being. We know, therefore, that there can be no absurdity in supposing that a being has more than one attribute, i.e., more than one essence. And if God is truly infinite, truly without any limitations whatever, we cannot suppose that he has only some finite number of attributes. So our conception of God as supremely perfect forces us to accept as legitimate the conception of a being possessing infinitely many attributes or essences.

Since this answer stays fairly close to what Spinoza in fact says, I cannot imagine that it will satisfy those who have thought long and hard about what Spinoza says and have not found *that* satisfactory. So let's approach the problem from a slightly different angle. Spinoza says that each of the attributes is conceived through itself (IP10). If each attribute is conceived through itself, must it not also exist in itself? If it existed in something else, i.e., needed something else in order to exist, wouldn't it (by IA4) have to be conceived through that thing? So we ought not to be surprised when Spinoza says he understands by *Natura naturans* (Nature considered as active)

> what is in itself and is conceived through itself, or such attributes of substance as express an eternal and infinite essence. (IP29S)

To say this is to say that the attributes of substance satisfy the definition of substance, they exist in themselves and are conceived through themselves (cf. KV I, vii, 10). But how can this be if there are many attributes and only one substance? Why should we think of these many attributes as constituting *one* substance, rather than many?

If we try to answer this by saying that, strictly speaking, substance is identical, not with any one attribute, but with the totality of its attributes—appealing, for example, to the definition of God as a substance consisting of infinite attributes (ID6), or to the language of IP19 or that of IP20C2—the reply may be that this is to treat the one "substance as an aggregate, a collection with members, or a complex with parts,"[37] and that we cannot ascribe to Spinoza any such view as that. Why not? Well, Spinoza conceives of substance as being indivisible (IP13) and says the notion of there being a part of substance involves a contradiction (IP13CS).

The problem is this: how can we remain true to Spinoza's language, which regularly speaks of substance as a complex, in which each of the attributes is an element, without suggesting that substance could somehow be decomposed into its various elements, or that some of these elements might exist apart from the others? The solution, so far as I can see, consists in recognizing that this particular complex is a complex of very special elements.[38] If each of the attributes not only is conceived through itself, but also exists in itself, then it exists without requiring the aid of any other thing. If it exists in *that* way, then its existence is necessary.[39] But if the existence of each of the attributes is necessary, then it is not possible that one of them should exist without the others. For if we said it was possible that one should exist without the others, that would imply that it was possible for the others not to exist. And that *isn't* really possible, not if each of the others exists in itself and is conceived through itself. The very self-sufficiency of each of the attributes, the fact that it is true of each of them that it does not need the others in order to exist, implies that there is no real possibility that at any time any one of them does exist without the others. The existence of each one of the attributes implies the existence of all the others.[40] Paraphrasing what Spinoza says in IP10S, all the attributes of substance have always been in it together. Since each of them, considered separately, exists in itself and is conceived through itself, they always *had* to be in it together.

12. WHAT DOES IT ALL MEAN?

If what I have maintained up to this point is correct, then Spinoza does have a powerful argument, from principles Descartes would have had difficulty rejecting, to the most uncartesian conclusion that there is only one substance, God. I don't claim at this point to have solved all of the problems that argument might involve. To take an obvious example: the answer I gave to the problem of the preceding section can only satisfy those troubled about the relation between the one substance and its many attributes if we can make sense of the claim that each of the attributes exists in itself, without requiring the aid of any other thing, and that its self-sufficiency is such as to make it reasonable to speak of its existing necessarily. I think we can. But before we attempt that, we need to touch ground again, to try to give the abstractions with which we have been wrestling some concrete meaning. It is one thing to deduce from Cartesian principles that there is, and must be, only one substance. It is another to understand this proposition.

If there is only one substance (IP14) and if everything else is a mode of that substance (IP15), then ordinary finite things must be modes of the one substance (IP25C). What on earth can this mean? The Cartesian metaphysic we have been using as our guide would suggest that it means that ordinary finite things are related to the one substance as thoughts are related to the thinker who has them, or size is related to the body that has it. This would be to say that ordinary finite things are predicable of the one substance as properties are predicable of a subject. But on the face of it, ordinary finite things are of the wrong logical type to be predicable of anything. What could it mean to say that a piece of wax was predicable of something? And what exactly would we be predicating it of?

In an earlier book on Spinoza, I took these questions to be hopelessly unanswerable and I proposed that we understand the relation of mode to substance, not as the inherence of a property in its subject, but as the relation of an effect to its cause.[41] I still think that's the most promising way to proceed, for reasons which will emerge as we go along (though I would claim to have already laid some ground for my reading in §6). But I would have to grant that the more traditional, alternative reading is not hopelessly unintelligible. We might argue, for example,[42] that for Spinoza, as for Descartes, ordinary physical objects are best viewed as larger or smaller portions of one continuous physical object, portions distinguishable from their neighbors only because they happen for a time to be qualitatively different. Ultimately there is just one extended thing, the whole of the physical universe (Descartes' "body in general"). The existence of lesser extended things just consists in the one extended thing's being qualified in certain ways at certain times and places. To say that the piece of wax is a mode of the one substance is to say that the one extended thing has certain properties at certain places and times (the places and times at which we would ordinarily say the wax exists).

Of course, the one extended thing is also God. And we might think that some of the properties we want to predicate of finite objects are odd properties to predicate of God—warmth, or fragrance, perhaps, in the case of the wax. But we can avoid that difficulty by recognizing that the properties we predicate of finite things need not be the same as the properties we would predicate of the one substance if we were to give a proper analysis of our predications of finite particular things. To say of a fight that it was protracted is really to say something about the men who were fighting, but not that they were protracted. Analogously, to say of the wax that it is fragrant is really to say something about the one extended thing, i.e., about God, but not necessarily that it is fragrant.

If we are worried that this analysis might commit us to predicating contradictory properties of God—since the one extended thing is hard in this place at this time, and not hard at that other place at this same time, or was fragrant here earlier, but is not fragrant here now—we can recognize that the temporal and spatial qualifiers render the apparent contradictions harmless.

This way of understanding Spinoza has enough textual support to be tempting, and to some extent perhaps it does represent something Spinoza held. In our exploration of Cartesian thought about substance we've seen that there certainly was a strong tendency in Descartes to say that really there is just one material substance, the whole of the physical world, and that the finite material things we ordinarily call substances are just modes of that one material substance.[43] As I read Descartes, this tendency never reaches the point of being a fully explicit and adequately articulated doctrine, but it's certainly there, and I think it may well have influenced Spinoza. There are places in Spinoza where he does speak as if his one substance were to be identified with the whole of Nature, and this fits in naturally with the view that the one extended substance is to be identified with the totality of physical things.[44]

But I do not think this way of understanding Spinoza gives us a reasonable account of the relation between substance and mode. One puzzle about this way of interpreting Spinoza is whether *any* of the properties we might be inclined to predicate of finite particulars is going to be properly predicable of the one substance. It's clear that properties like warmth and fragrance are not going to be fundamental enough to be predicable directly of substance, whatever we might think of the propriety of doing so. Spinoza, like Descartes, was an adherent of the 17th-century mechanistic program which tried to explain each thing's "secondary" qualities, its color, smell, temperature, etc., as being nothing more than functions of "primary" qualities, such as the size, shape and motion of the thing's constituent particles.[45] But would even the properties which are fundamental in Cartesio-Spinozistic physics be properly predicable of God? Size and shape are such properties, but Spinoza will not say that God has any particular size or shape (cf. IP15S, II / 57 / 4-12). Does adding spatial and temporal qualifiers—saying that God is spherical and has a volume of three cubic feet *here and now*—really make this predication acceptable to Spinoza? Being spherical and having a volume of three cubic feet are properties implying finiteness, hardly appropriate to an absolutely infinite being. Can they be made more appropriate by introducing further limitations?

But if properties as fundamental as size and shape are not properly predicable of God, what sorts of properties do underlie our ascriptions of more familiar properties to finite particulars? Do we have any idea?[46]

Again, it is hard to see how, following this line of thought, we can deny that God changes. When the wax changes, say, becomes softer on being carried nearer to the fire, according to this interpretation the one extended thing now has one property in one place and later has a contrary property in a different place. (It's not clear *what* property the extended thing has at these various times and places, but let that pass.) Doesn't it follow that the one extended thing changes? What more would it take for God to change? And yet it's clear that Spinoza will not allow that God can change (1P20C2).[47]

Another puzzle is what we are to make of those modes of substance which are not finite particulars. Spinoza develops the theory of these modes in 1PP21-23:

> P21: All the things which follow from the absolute nature of any of God's attributes have always had to exist and be infinite, or, are, through the same attribute, eternal and infinite.
>
> P22: Whatever follows from some attribute of God insofar as it is modified by a modification which, through the same attribute, exists necessarily and is infinite, must also exist and be infinite.
>
> P23: Every mode which exists necessarily and is infinite has necessarily had to follow either from the absolute nature of some attribute of God, or from some attribute, modified by a modification which exists necessarily and is infinite.

Writers on Spinoza customarily refer to these modes as the infinite modes, calling those which follow directly from the absolute nature of an attribute "immediate" infinite modes, and those which follow from the nature of an attribute as modified by an infinite mode "mediate" infinite modes. In the *Ethics* proper, Spinoza tells us precious little about these modes, and he does not have much more to say in other works. But we do learn in the correspondence (Letters 63 and 64) that absolutely infinite intellect is supposed to be an immediate infinite mode in the attribute of thought, that motion and rest is an immediate infinite mode in the attribute of extension, and that the body of the whole universe is a mediate mode, presumably in the attribute of extension.[48]

Now much of the doctrine of the infinite modes is extraordinarily obscure on any interpretation. It's a striking and important fact that there is no talk at all about infinite modes in Descartes.[49] But the doctrine of infinite modes becomes more puzzling than need be, on the interpretation we are presently considering. If the existence of a particular finite mode of extension is a matter of certain properties being predicable of the one extended thing at certain times and places, then presumably something analogous ought to be true of the infinite modes. Let's take the immediate infinite mode of extension— viz. motion and rest—since that's the infinite mode we probably have the best grasp of. Suppose the existence of this infinite mode is a matter of some property's being predicable of the one extended thing. Since this mode is infinite and eternal, the property we are speaking of will presumably not be predicable of the one extended thing at some particular times or places, but not others. It must be predicable of the extended thing as a whole, without spatial or temporal qualification. This property cannot be either the property of being in motion or that of being at rest. Only things with a location in space can be said to move or not to move. Space itself, or the whole of the universe, considered as an extended thing, does not have a location in space.[50] We have no idea what this property might be, but let that pass, since we are no better off regarding the properties underlying the finite modes. What we do know is that this property must be one which, in some sense, is caused by its subject. For if anything is clear in Spinoza it is that the one substance is supposed to be the cause of all of its modes, both finite and infinite. (See, for example, IP16 and its corollaries.) And one question which, on this interpretation, we ought to ask ourselves is: how can a subject cause itself to have the properties it has? how can the relation of inherence which a property has to its subject be anything like the relation an effect has to its cause?

13. A RADICAL SUGGESTION

Perhaps these questions are not unanswerable, but they are certainly difficult, and they suggest to me that it is unhelpful to think of the relation between mode and substance as a matter of a property's inhering in a thing (the whole of the universe), or, for that matter, to think of the one substance itself as the whole of the universe. It's certainly very natural to suppose that Spinoza identifies the one extended substance with the whole of the physical universe, and that he identifies the one substance itself with the whole of nature, not considered under any particular attribute. Popular expositions of Spinoza's thought often explain the self-sufficiency of substance by postulating this identification and then arguing that the whole of nature could not be dependent on anything external to it, since it encompasses everything that exists.[51] But where, exactly, does Spinoza argue in this fashion? And where, exactly, does he say that substance is the whole of nature?[52]

He does, of course, identify the one substance, God, with Nature, when he uses the famous phrase *Deus seu Natura* in the Preface to Part IV. Everyone agrees that this phrase should be translated "God or Nature," with the "or" being understood to represent some kind of equivalence between the two terms it links. But to what does the term "Nature" here refer? In IP29S Spinoza had already indicated that it is crucially ambiguous, between *natura naturans*, nature regarded as active, or

> what is in itself and is conceived through itself, or such attributes of substance as express eternal and infinite essence, i.e. God, insofar as he is considered as a free cause,

and *natura naturata*, nature regarded as passive, or

> whatever follows from the necessity of God's nature, or from any of God's attributes, or all the modes of God's attributes, insofar as they are considered as things which are in God, and which can neither be nor be conceived without God.

This suggests that Spinoza's well-known identification of God with Nature should be read as an identification of God with *natura naturans*, i.e., as an identification of substance with its attributes, an identification we have already found Spinoza making in his attempt to demonstrate that there is only one substance.[53]

What follows from the identification of substance with its attributes? One implication is that, when we ask what the relation is between a particular finite mode of substance and substance itself, what we are really asking is: what is the relation between a finite mode of an attribute of substance and the attribute of which it is the mode? And when we put the question that way, there should be much less temptation to think that the answer will take the form of showing how some thing, viz. the whole of the universe, can be thought of as having some property, we know not what.

This recasting of the question should come as no surprise to us. If we can form no clear concept of substance in abstraction from its attributes, then there will be nothing interesting to say about the relation between substance so conceived and its modes. To understand the relation between the mode and the substance we must conceive the substance under some attribute. That is, we must focus on the relation between the mode and the attribute it "expresses." This last term is Spinoza's own:

> Particular things are nothing but affections of God's attributes, or modes by which God's attributes are expressed in a certain and determinate way. (IP25C)

What is it for a mode to express an attribute?

The propositions which initiate the second half of Part I give us some important clues. One function they have is to explain in more detail what the relation between substance and mode consists in. P18D infers directly from the fact that all things are modes of God that they are caused by God. And the other propositions in this portion of Part I explain the nature of that causality. E.g., P16 tells us that

> an infinity of things must follow in infinite ways from the necessity of the divine nature . . .

and P17 adds that

> God acts solely from the laws of his own nature.

That is to say that God, considered as a free cause (P17C2) (= all of the attributes of substance, by P29S), produces and acts on things other than God (= the modes, both finite and infinite) in virtue of the laws of his own nature (= the laws of the attributes which constitute his nature, by D4), and that those things other than God must be understood to follow from those laws. One of the attributes which constitute the nature of substance is extension. So we must think of extension as involving certain laws—to borrow a rare Spinozistic metaphor from the *Treatise on the Intellect* (§101) we must think of the attributes as having laws "inscribed in them, as in their true codes"—and we must think of the infinite modes of extension, and of particular finite bodies, as following from those laws.

14. CARTESIAN PHYSICS

We will be helped to understand this, I think, if we recall the extremely important role the laws of nature play in the Cartesian attempt to deduce physics from metaphysics. The central concept of Cartesian physics is the concept of motion. The essence of a body is to be an extended thing, to be a thing with size and shape. But Descartes cannot proceed very far in the explanation of the other properties of material things until he attributes motion to them. Thus Cartesian physics explains the difference between hot and cold bodies in terms of the differences in the motion of their constituent particles; it explains the differences between bodies of different colors in terms of the differences in the motion imparted to the minute particles reflected from their surface when they are illuminated by rays of light; and so on. All changes in what later philosophers were to call secondary qualities (heat, color, smell, etc.) are to be explained in terms of changes in such primary qualities as size, shape and motion, and the most important of these primary qualities is motion. This project of explaining all other properties of bodies in terms of their mechanical properties has been called "the mechanization of the world picture" and in one form or another all the "new philosophers" of the 17th century subscribed to it.

But why do bodies move? It is not their nature to do so. Their essence is simply to be extended things. They move because God imparts motion to them. God is the primary cause of motion. Note that I say God imparts motion to them, not that in the beginning of the world he imparted it to them. Descartes does not conceive of God as initiating, at the creation, a motion which bodies have subsequently sustained of themselves. Creation is continuous. Finite things are so dependent on God that they could not even continue to exist from one moment to the next if they were not sustained by God.

But God's implication in the motions of finite things, in the context of traditional theology, creates certain problems for Descartes. God is supposed to be supremely perfect, and this implies that he is an eternal, immutable being. If a perfect being were to change, it could only change for the worse. But if God is immutable, cannot change, how can he be the continuous cause of a constantly changing world?

Descartes' solution is to make the laws of nature an intermediary between God and the finite world. If God is the primary cause of motion, the "secondary and particular causes of the different motions which we notice in individual bodies" (*Principles* II, 37) are the laws of nature. Descartes identifies three laws as particularly fundamental:

> 1. Each thing, insofar as it can, always remains in the same state, and does not change unless acted on by external causes.
> 2. Every motion, of itself, is always in a straight line, so that deviations from rectilinear motion must always be due to some external cause.

These first two laws amount to a version of the principle of inertia. Together they tell us that things will not change unless something acts on them. It is Descartes' third law which explains how bodies interact, and hence how change occurs in the physical world:

> 3. If a moving body comes in contact with another body which has more motion than it does, it will not impart any motion to the other body, but will only change the direction of its own motion; but if it comes in contact

with another body which has less motion than it does, it will move the other body along with it, and impart to it as much of its own motion as it loses.

Descartes' third law implies that, in any interaction between bodies, the total quantity of motion is preserved. Having laid down these fundamental laws, Descartes proceeds to deduce other, less general laws from them, laws he claims will be capable of accounting for all the phenomena of the physical world.

Although the world is in a constant state of flux, God's action on the world is constant. If one body, for example, starts to move because another, moving body comes into contact with it, God's role in causing this event consists simply in his establishing the law according to which this is what happens in this type of situation. Since the law is eternal and immutable, God's eternity and immutability are not compromised.

15. SOLUTIONS GENERATE NEW PROBLEMS

Descartes' solution to the problem of reconciling God's continuous creation of a constantly changing world with his own immutability is a brilliant one, but not without problems of its own.[54] What exactly is the status of these laws of nature? Descartes calls them eternal truths, which, in the language of 17th-century philosophy, implies that they are necessary truths; and he professes to deduce them from God's immutability, which would confirm their necessity. It is supposed to be a necessary truth about God that he is immutable; and what follows logically from a necessary truth must itself be necessary. But the postulation of a set of eternal laws of nature invites awkward theological questions.

Descartes' remarks about the essence of material things in the Fifth Meditation prompted Gassendi to ask whether it was not a serious matter to set up an eternal and immutable nature in addition to and independent of God (AT VII, 319). In reply Descartes said he did not conceive of the eternal truths as being independent of God. Rather God had established them as a king might establish the laws of his kingdom. So they depend on the will of God, and are eternal and immutable only because the will of God is eternal and immutable (AT VII, 380-382, 435-436). This is the famous doctrine of the creation of the eternal truths.

Spinoza, I think, regarded this as precisely what it is, a fundamentally incoherent position. Descartes wanted to have it both ways. Cartesian science requires the laws of nature to be necessary truths, as a condition of the intelligibility of nature and the possibility of science. The laws of nature are supposed to be the same in any world God might have created and to hold immutably in the world he did create. But Cartesian theology requires the laws of nature to be contingent truths, rigorously subordinated to the will of an arbitrary creator, who might have imposed very different laws on his creation, and who might, at any time, change his decrees, since they have to be conceived as not following from God's essence in order to be conceived as contingent (cf. E IP17S, P33S2, IIP3S).

16. SPINOZISTIC PHYSICS: THE ATTRIBUTES

Recognizing the impossibility of Descartes' attempt at compromise, Spinoza made the natural choice for a philosopher committed to the intelligibility of nature.[55] He rejected the notion of God as a personal creator and identified God with (the attributes in which are inscribed) the fundamental laws of nature, which provide the ultimate explanation for everything that happens in nature. That is, *he identified God with Nature, not conceived as the totality of things, but conceived as the most general principles of order exemplified by things.*[56] If

you do not find this as explicit as you might like it to be in Part
I of the *Ethics*, consider what Spinoza writes in the Preface of
Part III:

> Nature [= *natura naturans*] is always the same, and its
> virtue and power of acting are everywhere one and the
> same; that is, the laws and rules of Nature, according to
> which all things happen and all things are changed from
> one form into another. That is why there must also be one
> and the same way of understanding the nature of any-
> thing whatever, viz., through the universal laws and rules
> of Nature. (II / 138)

Given Spinoza's identification of God with *natura naturans*
(in IP29S), and his identification of God's power with his essence (in IP34), we have here a thoroughly naturalistic explanation of Spinoza's claim that God's essence, i.e. the totality
of his attributes, is eternal (P19) and immutable (P20C2). The
eternality and immutability of God's essence *is* the eternality
and immutability of the fundamental laws of nature. What
Descartes had called the secondary cause of motion, the laws
of extended nature, become the primary cause of motion.

But not without reason. Quite apart from the internal difficulties of the Cartesian attempt at compromise, it makes a
good deal of sense to think of these fundamental laws of nature as God. Once we give up the pseudo-explanation involved in explaining the most fundamental laws of nature in
terms of the will of an omnipotent person, those laws do provide the ultimate explanation of events in the world, in the
sense that once we have led events back to those laws, there is
no further that we can go. They are also ultimate in a deeper
sense, in that there are logical reasons why we should not expect to be able to go further.

Explanation, in Cartesian science, is deductive. We explain
the particular by deducing it from the general, or the less gen-

eral by deducing it from the more general. For example, it is, according to Cartesian physics, a general principle that if two bodies of equal size, moving at equal speeds in opposite directions, collide, they will each reverse their directions and maintain the same speed they previously had. (*Principles* II, 46) And that is supposed to be explained by being deduced from the more general principle that the total quantity of motion is preserved in all cases of impact. But if extension really is a concept of maximal generality, then it is in the nature of extension that there can be no explanation for laws governing all extended things. Once you have led your explanation of physical laws back to a principle dealing with all bodies, without qualification, there can be no more fundamental principle which will explain that principle. So the unavailability of an explanation for these most fundamental laws is quite unlike the unavailability of an explanation for some less general principle or some particular fact. If there is some particular fact we are unable to explain—say, why this ball shot from a cannon traces the parabolic path it does—the particularity of that fact encourages us to think that, like other facts of that level of generality, it must ultimately be explainable. Failures to find an explanation are failures to find something which we have reason to believe should be there to be found. But a failure to find an explanation for facts so general that we cannot conceive of any more general facts from which they might be deduced is a failure of a logically different kind, a failure to find something it would be logically impossible to find.

If this is correct, then we can look on the fundamental laws of nature not only as principles which explain whatever happens in nature, but also as principles which themselves could not, by their very nature, be explained by anything else. I think Spinoza would have regarded that as sufficient ground for thinking that they must be self-explanatory. That everything which exists must have a reason or cause why it exists is one of his deepest assumptions (cf. IA3, P8S, PIID2). It's also an assumption he shared with Descartes (cf. AT VII, 164-165). If the fundamental laws of nature can't, precisely because they are so fundamental, be explained by anything else, then we must regard them as self-explanatory. There is, *and could have been*, nothing other than the fundamental laws themselves which caused them to be what they are. So there is, *and could have been*, nothing which, had it been different, would have led to their being different. But if there are no conceivable circumstances under which they would have been otherwise—no circumstances conceivable by any intellect, not merely no circumstances conceivable by a finite human intellect—then what sense would there be in saying that they could have been otherwise? They could not have been otherwise. This gives a reasonable sense to the notion of God as a self-sufficient, necessary being, and makes good on the promissory note issued at the beginning of §12.

17. SPINOZISTIC PHYSICS: THE INFINITE MODES

The attributes exist in themselves, are self-sufficient, in the sense that the laws "inscribed in them" are not, and *could not be*, the consequences of any more general principles. The infinite and finite modes, I say, follow from the attributes. In the case of at least one of the infinite modes, motion and rest, we have a tolerably clear idea what that mode's "following" from the attribute might consist in.

There are laws of motion and rest, principles which apply to all bodies which are in motion or at rest, principles which are deducible from the laws of extension, i.e., from principles which apply to all extended things without qualification. These laws of motion and rest in turn serve as the principles of explanation for more particular facts, i.e., for laws of lesser generality and for particular happenings in nature. These laws are infinite in the same sense that the laws involved in the attributes are: they apply throughout nature, without limitation to any particular time and place. They are eternal in the sense that their existence is necessary. But the nature of the necessity here is not quite the same as that possessed by the attributes. The attributes involve principles which, for purely logical reasons, could not have a cause and could not have been otherwise. The infinite modes involve principles which do have a cause and could have been otherwise, *if* that cause could have been otherwise. But that cause could not have been otherwise. So they are necessary, but their necessity is derivative from that of the attributes.[57]

Spinoza gives us a sketch of the deduction of these subordinate laws in the digression on physics after E IIP13 (II / 97 / 19-103 / 5), when he states certain general principles applying to all extended objects:

> A1′: All bodies either move or are at rest;
> A2′: Each body moves, now more slowly, now more quickly;

and claims to derive from them (with the help of his metaphysics, most notably, IP28) a version of one of the fundamental laws of Cartesian physics, the principle of inertia:

> L3C: A body in motion moves until it is determined by another body to rest; and a body at rest also remains at rest until it is determined to motion by another. (II / 98 / 24)

But this is only a draft of a Spinozistic physics, and is very incomplete. E.g., it contains no principle corresponding fully to Descartes' third law of motion. Spinoza includes this much of a physics in his *Ethics* because he believes he needs to give at least a rudimentary account of the nature of the human body before he tries to explain the nature of the human mind. It appears to have been his intention to work out a more thorough and systematic physics. But he never lived to complete that work, and one of the last letters we have from him confesses that he has not yet been able to get his thoughts in proper order on the problems of physics (Letter 83, IV / 334 / 22-28). The doctrine of the infinite modes, on this interpretation, is an affirmation of faith that that project could, in principle, be completed, that it must, for metaphysical reasons, be capable of completion.

18. SPINOZISTIC PHYSICS: THE FINITE MODES

Spinoza uses rather special language to describe the relation between God's attributes and the infinite modes: he says that they follow from the *absolute* nature of those attributes (1PP21,23). But the *finite* modes do not follow from the absolute nature of the attributes (1P28D), i.e., they do not follow unconditionally from the attributes, as the infinite modes do. That is why the finite modes are not infinite and eternal, why they are particular things, which have a finite and determinate existence (1P28), i.e., which come into being and pass away.[58]

I take this as a representation, within the terms of Spinoza's metaphysics, of the fact that, even if the most ambitious dreams of science are realized, there are limits to what a unified science could do in explaining the detail of the world. Suppose that all the laws of nature can indeed be organized into a deductive system in which a few fundamental principles generate all the rest. In order to apply those laws to concrete situations, to explain, say, why this particular body is moving in the particular direction and with the particular speed that it is, we need to understand not only the laws of motion, but also the prior interactions of that body with other bodies. And to understand the motions of those other bodies, we need to understand *their* prior interactions with still other bodies.[59] That is why we get 1P28:

> Every singular thing, or any thing which is finite and has a determinate existence, can neither exist nor be determined to produce an effect unless it is determined to exist and produce an effect by another cause, which is also finite and has a determinate existence; and again, this cause also can neither exist nor be determined to produce an effect unless it is determined to exist and produce an effect by another, which is also finite and has a determinate existence, and so on to infinity.

The dependence of finite particulars on an infinite series of other finite particulars does not, of course, mean that they are not also dependent on God. Whatever exists and produces any effect, whether finite or infinite, must have been determined by God to exist and produce that effect (1P26). In terms of the interpretation here advanced, this is to say that to understand finite particulars—the motion of this particular body, at this particular speed, in this particular direction—we must appeal not only to the other finite particulars which conditioned them, but also to the laws of nature. The finite modes follow from, are deducible from, a finite series of infinite causes, the laws of nature, taken in conjunction with an infinite series of finite causes, the other, prior finite modes. That is, the finite modes follow from God's attributes (via the infinite modes), but do not follow from God's nature absolutely, only conditionally.[60]

19. THE NECESSITY OF ALL THINGS

My attempt to explain how all things could be modes of one substance is now essentially complete. I have argued that we must think of the relation between a mode and the one substance as a relation between that mode and the attribute of which it is a mode, and that modes exist in substance in the sense that they follow, in different ways, from the attributes of substance. There is, in my interpretation, a good sense in which there is nothing contingent in nature (1P29): the most general features of the universe, that is, the laws involved in the attributes of substance, are necessary in the sense that they could not have had a cause distinct from themselves, and hence, could not have been otherwise; other, less general features of the universe, the infinite modes in which are inscribed the subordinate laws of nature, could not have been otherwise because they follow from features of the universe which, in their own right, could not have been otherwise; and particular features of the universe, the finite modes which we might think of as particular facts in nature, could not have been otherwise because they follow from the general features of the universe in conjunction with other particular features of the universe.

Because these particular features of the universe—such as the fact that a particular body is moving from a certain place, in a certain direction, at a certain time—do not follow *unconditionally* from the general features of the universe, it may be felt that this introduces an unacceptable element of contingency into Spinoza's view of the world. Considered in themselves, apart from the causes which determine them to be what they are, these particular features of the universe are contingent, could have been otherwise. And that may be felt to be unacceptable in a rigorously deterministic system. If each particular feature of the universe, considered in itself, is contingent, then their totality is also contingent, and there is at least one thing which does not have an explanation: the totality of particular features of the universe.[61] But if this is felt to be unacceptable, perhaps that is because we have placed demands on Spinoza's system which it was never intended to satisfy. Spinoza certainly takes a kind of contingency to be axiomatic (cf. E IIAI). He certainly makes a distinction between the different senses in which a thing may be necessary and does not think that all things are necessary in the same sense (1P33S1; cf. CM I, iii). Equally certainly, the determinism here attributed to him is strong enough to be philosophically interesting and to bear the weight of the moral conclusions Spinoza wants to draw from it.

But that is properly a theme for the chapters which follow. Here it must suffice to conclude that Spinoza's monism, his doctrine that there is only one substance, of which everything else is a mode, turns out to be a form of the doctrine of determinism, and hence to be as intelligible and defensible as that particular form of determinism is. This seems to me not a trifling conclusion.

II

On Man

I. METHOD AGAIN

IN THE FIRST chapter I announced, as a general theme for this book, the attempt to penetrate behind the geometric method. The *Ethics* is a peculiarly difficult work to read, largely because of its axiomatic form. Descartes was right about one thing, at least: metaphysics does not lend itself as readily to that style of presentation as mathematics does. (AT VII, 156-157) Its central concepts are too abstract, and too difficult to get clear about, for an axiomatic text in metaphysics to be as readily intelligible as Euclid's *Geometry*. And so I suggested that one useful way of approaching the *Ethics* is to try to reconstruct the dialogue in which Spinoza was engaged with his predecessors, and which he suppressed in his exposition because of his distaste for appearing to attack particular individuals (IV / 8 / 18, 72 / 28). If I was right in the interpretation I offered last time, then critical reflection on the philosophy of Descartes has much to offer us in the understanding of Spinoza.

Now I have another interpretive suggestion to make. When I first attempted to understand Spinoza's *Ethics*, some twenty-five years ago, I recall being put off by the formal apparatus. There was Spinoza, very conscientiously explaining to me how he wished the central notions of his system to be understood, and I didn't understand the definitions. The terms he used to define the terms he wanted me to understand often seemed as obscure as the terms they were used to define. And

I felt that if I couldn't understand the definitions, or the axioms which used the same concepts, then I couldn't hope to understand the theorems derived from them.

In retrospect, I now think that this is a very natural, but a very mistaken reaction. Spinoza's initial definitions are not immediately intelligible, any more than his axioms are all as immediately obvious as the parallel with Euclid would encourage us to think they should be. But it is not true that we must first have a firm grasp of Spinoza's initial assumptions before we can understand what follows them. Often we can get more of the sense of a formula by seeing what follows from it, or what Spinoza thinks follows from it, than we can by focussing all of our attention on the formula itself. To illustrate this, let us consider Spinoza's account of what man is.

2. CARTESIAN ANTHROPOLOGY

As before, we may begin by reconstructing the Cartesian account against which, I would contend, Spinoza was reacting. In the first chapter we saw that Descartes conceived the world as consisting of two radically distinct kinds of substances: minds and bodies, minds being thinking, non-extended substances, and bodies being extended, non-thinking substances. There are, as we noted, some passages which suggest a tendency to reduce the number of material substances to one, but Descartes' most usual position is that there are many material substances, and for the sake of simplicity, we can speak as if that were Descartes' only position.

Descartes' official position is also that human beings are composite substances, whose constituent substances are minds and bodies. I, Edwin Curley, am not one thing, but two: a mind and a body, both of which co-exist in that peculiarly close kind of relationship which Descartes called "substantial union." Considered in themselves, my mind and my body are "complete substances," in the sense that each can be conceived to exist without the other, or without anything else except God. But my mind and my body need not be considered simply as isolated things. They can also be considered in relation to the whole human being they constitute.[1] The union which joins a human body to a human soul is essential to the human being; without it a man is not a man (K, 130).

Descartes makes it a good deal easier to see how mind and body can be considered as distinct complete substances than he does to see how they can be considered as constituting one thing, so let's look first at the doctrine of real distinction before discussing the doctrine of substantial union.

3. THE REAL DISTINCTION BETWEEN MIND AND BODY

That bodies can be conceived as existing without minds may seem, nowadays, too obvious to need proof. In fact, however, Descartes felt that many physicists—notably the Scholastics—were committed to attributing to bodies properties which it would make sense to ascribe to them only if they possessed minds. E.g., in explaining the fact that wine will not flow from an opening in the bottom of a cask when the top is completely closed, they appealed to the notion of a fear of a vacuum. But, Descartes says, "we are well aware that the wine has no mind to fear anything; and even if it did, I do not know for what reason it could be apprehensive of this vacuum, which indeed is nothing but a chimera" (AT XI, 20). For similar reasons he rejected as absurd Roberval's suggestion that each particle of matter in the universe has a property in virtue of which all are drawn towards each other and attract each other in their turn:

> In order to make sense of this one would have to suppose not only that each particle of matter had a soul . . . , but

also that these souls were conscious, and indeed, divine, to be able to know without any intermediary what was happening in those distant places, and to exercise their powers there . . . (Letter to Mersenne, 20 April 1646, K 191)

Would pointing out the need to assume a soul in every particle of matter be enough in itself to reduce Roberval's hypothesis to absurdity?

However we answer that last question, I suggest that part of the point of the analysis of the piece of wax in the Second Meditation is to show us that we can conceive of bodies simply as extended things, capable of change with respect to the particular properties which give expression to their general, geometrical nature, but not possessing any properties which smack of thought. The program of Cartesian physics, for which the analysis of the wax is intended to prepare us, involves showing that these inherently intelligible geometrical properties suffice for the explanation of all other observable properties of bodies (*Principles* II, 64). Although Cartesian physics did ascribe a "striving after motion" (*conatus ad motum*) to bodies, Descartes was anxious that this concept should be understood antiseptically, as not implying any thought on the part of the moving body (*Principles* III, 56).

The converse proposition—that minds can be conceived as existing without bodies—is clearly not so obvious as not to require proof. But Descartes thinks it is demonstrated by the argument of the first two Meditations. The First Meditation shows me that I can conceive of the possibility that no bodies exist, the possibility that their appearance to me as existing is a mere illusion, generated by my mind's capacity for dreaming or by the activities of an omnipotent deceiving spirit. But the Second Meditation shows that I cannot at the same time conceive of my mind's not existing—not consistently, at any rate.

For the hypotheses I entertained in order to doubt the existence of the external world, and would have to entertain in order to doubt my mind's existence, imply that my mind exists. If I dream that I am sitting by the fire, when I am really in bed, then I think. And if I think, I exist. If a demon deceives me into thinking that I exist in a world of extended objects, then I think. And once again, if I think, I exist. Any hypothesis I entertain to cast doubt on any belief must have the form "Perhaps you are mistaken because . . ." In doing so, it will imply my existence, at least to the extent that I conceive of myself simply as a thinking thing.[2] The first two Meditations are, among other things, a thought experiment designed to demonstrate the possibility of my conceiving of myself simply as a thinking thing, that is, to demonstrate the possibility of conceiving a mind as existing without there being any body.

By the end of the *Meditations* Descartes evidently takes himself to have shown something stronger than the mere conceptual possibility of the mind's existing apart from the body. There seem to be two reasons for this. First, if I have been created by a God who is not a deceiver, then whatever I conceive clearly and distinctly, that is, conceive in such a way that I cannot help so conceiving it, must be true. So if my conception that I might exist without the existence of any body is clear and distinct, then it must really be at least logically possible for me so to exist, i.e., it must be true that this conception does not involve any contradiction. Secondly, if God exists and is omnipotent, then there is a power in the universe capable of giving reality to any logical possibility. So no logical possibility is a *mere* logical possibility.

Up to a point Descartes' dualism provides philosophical support for the orthodox Christian belief in the immortality of the soul: insofar as we think of the mind or soul simply as a thing that thinks, it is something which *could* survive the death of the body; the possibility of immortality cannot be foreclosed by any argument based on the soul's metaphysical status. We can, with a good intellectual conscience, accept the hope offered us by the Church. But Descartes' arguments for the real distinction between mind and body also lead him to speak frequently in a way apt to arouse theological opposition, to speak as if *he*, René Descartes, were really nothing but a mind, and not the composite of mind and body which his official position proclaims him to be.[3] The self whose existence is proven by the famous *cogito* argument is a self whose essential nature is to be a thinking thing.

4. THE SUBSTANTIAL UNION

Descartes does not want to leave matters thus. Late in the *Meditations*, after his arguments have assured him that he need not fear deception by the Evil Spirit and can trust his clear and distinct ideas, and after he has established that the material world does indeed exist, Descartes begins to explore his relationship to that one body which is peculiarly his:

> Nature teaches me, through those sensations of pain, hunger, thirst, etc., that I am not only present in my body as a sailor [FV: pilot] is present in his ship,[4] but that I am very closely conjoined to it, and as it were, mingled throughout it, so that together with it I compose one thing. For otherwise, when the body is injured, I who am [would be?] nothing other than a thinking thing, would not feel pain on its account, but would perceive that injury by pure intellect, as a sailor perceives by vision if something is broken in his ship; and when the body required food or drink, I would understand this explicitly, I would not have those confused sensations of hunger and thirst. For certainly, those sensations of thirst, hunger, pain, etc., are nothing but certain confused modes of

thinking, which have arisen from the union, and as it were, thorough mingling of the mind with the body. (AT VII, 81)

This passage has given rise to much controversy. Burman, a young student who interviewed Descartes towards the end of his life, was prompted by it to ask how two things whose natures are so completely different could act on one another (C, 28; AT V, 163). And he was only one among many of Descartes' contemporaries to raise this issue. Princess Elisabeth too was moved to ask how the soul, being immaterial and non-extended, could move the body.[5] The assumption seems to be that motion in a body can be caused only by contact with another moving body.

When Descartes was pressed on this topic, as he was repeatedly, the best answer he seems to have been able to give was to say something like this: of course, it is difficult to understand how a non-extended thing can cause an extended thing to move; but experience assures us *that* it happens, so we must not doubt that; as for understanding *how* it happens, the best we can do is to say that we have a primitive concept of the union of the mind with the body, of their constituting together one thing, and that it is in virtue of this union that the mind is able to act on the body and conversely; this notion of the substantial union of mind and body is a primitive one, which cannot be satisfactorily explained in terms of any other more basic concept; it is thus on a par with the notions of thought and extension, which are the primitive notions corresponding to our concepts of mind and body considered as separate entities; and so it is intelligible enough in its own right.[6]

Now I think you can understand why subsequent philosophers would not have found this very satisfactory. To appeal to a primitive, unanalyzable concept in order to explain something admitted to be mysterious amounts to throwing up one's hands in despair. And it is natural to wonder how the talk of mind and body as constituting together one thing is supposed to comport with the doctrine that they are really distinct substances, each capable of existing apart from the other.

On the other hand, it does seem to me that Descartes grasped certain facts about our experience which anyone philosophizing about the relationship between mind and body had better acknowledge, and which his doctrine of substantial union is an attempt to articulate. One of these facts is that I am aware of what happens in my body in a very special way. I have an awareness of what happens in my body which extends throughout the whole of my body and which is not mediated by any of the sense organs through which I become aware of the world external to my body. As I compose this paragraph, I am sitting at my desk looking out the window at nothing in particular. The view from my window is not very exciting. But as I stare into space, I am very much aware of the position of my legs, feet, arms and hands, of a slight itching sensation in my neck, of sensations of hunger and thirst, and so on.

Whatever my relationship to my body is, these basic bodily sensations indicate that it is a relationship to my whole body, and not just to some part of it.[7] And while it may be awkward for Descartes to express this relationship in terms which suggest that the mind is a physical, extended thing—as he does when he says metaphorically that the mind is, as it were, mingled throughout the body (AT VII, 81)—perhaps that is a sign that we ought not to insist too strongly on the supposed fact that the mind is non-extended. It may be that we can conceive of the mind as engaging in thinking without being required to think of it as extended. But perhaps this conceptual fact is misleading about the true nature of the mind. When Elisabeth wrote that it was easier to attribute matter and extension to the soul than to attribute to it the capacity to move a body, and to be moved by it, without having matter, Descartes replied (28 June 1643) that she should feel free to attribute matter and extension to the soul, "for that is nothing but conceiving it as being united to the body" (K, 142-143)!

The other fact is that I have an immediate, unreasoning concern for my body, for its integrity and for its various needs. To put it a bit perversely, I take a very personal interest in my body. If my body is damaged or in need of something, I have a natural tendency to act to do something about that damage or that need. Desires and actions prompted by basic bodily sensations are fundamental to my nature and are a sure indication that my relation to my body is not merely an external one. It is difficult to express this without sounding dualistic. To talk about my relation to my body—to say, as I did a moment ago, that I take a very personal interest in my body—is to talk as if my body were something distinct from myself. The language we have created for the discussion of these problems is so permeated with dualistic assumptions, that we can hardly formulate a non-dualistic position without sounding paradoxical. But what I really want to say is that, in some sense, I and my body are one. That is why I have the concern for it that I do and why I have the awareness of it that I have. That is the metaphysical truth which Descartes was trying to express when he denied that his relation to his body was like that of a sailor to his ship.

However hard it may be to express these intuitions, I take it that Descartes and Spinoza shared them, and that these intuitions were more important in the genesis of the Spinozistic position than any concerns about the intelligibility of interaction between distinct substances.[8] Descartes wants to convey a sense of the unity between mind and body, so he talks about the substantial union of mind and body. But he also wants to allow for the possibility of the mind's continuing in existence after the death of the body. That seems to him at least a conceptual possibility, and he is convinced that the existence of an omnipotent being renders all conceptual possibilities real possibilities. Once again he is trying to have things both ways. We cannot conceive of human beings as composite substances, compounded of two radically distinct entities, and still conceive of them as constituting one being in the way required to do justice to the facts of our experience.

5. SPINOZISTIC ANTHROPOLOGY

If the key proposition of Part I of the *Ethics*—the proposition which is at once most distinctively Spinozistic, richest in systematic connections, and most puzzling as regards its meaning and rationale—is P14, the claim that God is the only substance, then the key proposition of Part II is not a proposition at all, but a statement made all too casually in a scholium occurring almost exactly at the mid-point of this part of the *Ethics*:

> The mind and the body are one and the same individual, which is conceived now under the attribute of thought, now under the attribute of extension. (IIP21S)

Spinoza holds that this statement follows[9] from a more famous statement made in an earlier scholium: "A mode of extension and the idea of that mode are one and the same thing, but expressed in two ways" (IIP7S). But while the earlier statement may be more fundamental, in the sense that it is more general, and has more far-reaching implications, the later statement joins issue with Descartes more sharply and clearly.

As I read Spinoza, he is responding to the tension I have described between the Cartesian doctrine of real distinction and the Cartesian doctrine of substantial union. He began, I suggest, by being deeply puzzled by Descartes' notion that the mind and body are "substantially united." If this was supposed to imply that the human mind and the human body, though each a substance in its own right, nevertheless combined to form yet a third substance, it could not be right. Quite apart from any argument based on their dependence on God, it was manifest that neither the mind nor the body possessed the kind of independence of other finite things which its being a substance would require.[10] Nevertheless, the facts of human experience which led Descartes to formulate that doctrine could not be denied. There is a particular body, a human body, to which the human mind has a peculiarly intimate relationship: we know immediately that it is affected in certain ways (IIA4); we do not have analogous knowledge of any other body; rather, whatever knowledge we have of any other particular body must be mediated by the immediate awareness we have of the body we call our own (IIP26); and the special awareness we have of this body extends throughout the whole of that body, it is not restricted to any particular part of it (IIP12); in particular, we are aware, through the sensation of pain, if any part of the body is injured. These facts make it reasonable for Descartes to have spoken of the mind as being "as it were intermingled with the body," however awkward the spatial metaphor might be for his dualism. They make it reasonable for us to say, at least, that the mind is united to the body in the sense that it is the idea of the body.[11]

Spinoza has, of course, a metaphysical argument which shows to his satisfaction the impossibility of describing things as Descartes usually does. If it pertains to the nature of substance to exist necessarily (IPP7, 11), and if no human being exists necessarily (IIA1), then a human being cannot be a substance (IIP10).[12] If there is only one substance (IP14), then a human being cannot be a composite of two substances. Moreover, Spinoza's metaphysic suggests an alternative, happier way of characterizing the situation. If there is an extended

substance (as there must be, since there are modes of extension—E IIP2), and if there is a thinking substance (as, again,
there must be, since there are modes of thought—E IIP1), and
if there is really only one substance (E IP14), which has all
possible attributes (IP10), then the extended substance and the
thinking substance must be one and the same substance,
which is now understood in one way, now in another, depending on the attribute in terms of which it is conceived (IIP7S). It
follows, Spinoza thinks,[13] that a mode of extension and the
idea of that mode must be one and the same thing, expressed
in two ways (IIP7S). What could better explain the mind's peculiarly close relationship to this one body, its awareness of
what happens to this body, its concern for this body's needs,
its dependence on its awareness of this body for its awareness
of all other bodies, than to say that the mode of extension with
which the human mind is identical is this particular human
body?

6. PARALLELISM

This, I think, is the question which lies at the heart of Spinoza's theory of mind-body identity. But there is one crucial link
in the argument of the preceding paragraph which cries out
for a more searching examination. Let's suppose, for the sake
of argument, at least, that we are satisfied with Spinoza's demonstrations of the main propositions of Part I of the *Ethics*.
This means, in particular, that we are satisfied that there can
be only one substance, that that substance must be absolutely
infinite, in the sense that it lacks nothing which involves any
perfection, and that if there is a thinking substance and an
extended substance, *they must be the same substance*. Let's
suppose also that we accept the first two propositions of Part
II: there is a thinking substance and there is an extended substance. Does it really follow from this that every mode of the
thinking substance must be identical with some mode of the

extended substance and conversely? Why should not the thinking substance have some modes which are not identical with any mode of the extended substance? Why should not the extended substance have some modes which are not identical with any mode of the thinking substance? Why should *any* mode of the thinking substance be identical with a mode of extension? Why should *any* mode of the extended substance be identical with a mode of thought?[14]

These seem to me to be fair, but difficult questions. Let's approach them by asking something which I think may be a bit easier. If the identity theses questioned above are true, then there must at least be a one-to-one correspondence between modes of thought and modes of extension, in the sense that, for every mode of thought which has a mode of extension as its object, there must be a corresponding mode of extension and conversely. (In saying that there must *at least* be such a one-to-one correspondence, I mean that talk of a "correspondence" between modes of thought and modes of extension should not be taken to prejudge the issue of identity. It implies neither identity nor non-identity.) Why might Spinoza have thought that there must be such a correspondence?

Commentators usually look to IIP7 for the definitive statement of the doctrine of parallelism:

> P7: The order and connection of ideas is the same as the order and connection of things.

Spinoza's demonstration of this proposition is maddeningly brief:

> This is clear from IA4. For the idea of each thing caused depends on the knowledge of the cause of which it is the effect.

That's the whole of it. Now I agree with those commentators who don't find this demonstration very helpful.[15] IA4 had said that knowledge of an effect depends on and involves knowledge of its cause. Spinoza's paraphrase in P7D substitutes the term "idea" for the term "knowledge" in its first occurrence, a common equivalence in Spinoza, which I don't propose to puzzle over here. The central problem with this demonstration is that it will generate a correspondence between thought and extension only if there are some modes of thought to begin with: *if* there is an idea of an effect, then there must be an idea of its cause, and there must be a relation of dependence between them. But why must there be an idea of the effect?

The answer seems to be that Spinoza is relying on IIP3 to carry much of the weight of the doctrine of parallelism.[16] IIP3 gives us one-half of the correspondence: it implies that there is a mode of thought corresponding to every mode of extension. Spinoza never states the converse of that: that there is a mode of extension for every mode of thought. In my view he shouldn't state it because he doesn't believe it. What he does believe is a more restricted proposition: there is a mode of extension for every idea which has a mode of extension as its object.

For Spinoza not every mode of thought has for its object some mode of extension. Quite apart from the fact that some modes of thought have a mode of thought for their object (see IIPP20-23), there are in thought ideas of objects in attributes other than thought and extension, attributes which are unknown to us. We do not perceive any singular things except bodies and modes of thinking (IIA5). The reason why we don't perceive modes of the unknown attributes is that our minds are essentially ideas of modes of extension (IIP11, P13) and not ideas of modes of the other attributes. But there are, in the attribute of thought, ideas of the modes of those unknown attributes, ideas which constitute the minds of those objects. Because the *Ethics* says little or nothing explicitly about the unknown attributes, it seems a permissible simplification to neglect them in what follows. They are very mysterious. In discussing Spinoza's parallelism, I shall acknowledge the existence of these other attributes, and of ideas of their modes, by the way I qualify my statement of the one-to-one correspondence: that there is a mode of thought for every mode of extension and that there is a mode of extension for every mode of thought *which has as its object a mode of extension.* But I shall not undertake any further discussion of them.[17]

Why might Spinoza think that the doctrine of parallelism, so understood, must be true? The proof he offers of IIP3 seems to me more obscure than the proposition itself, insofar as it involves an appeal to IP35, which is very difficult to interpret.[18] I don't propose to spend any time puzzling about that argument, since I think a different, and (I hope) more persuasive, argument has deeper roots in Spinoza's thought.[19] That more fundamental argument might be stated as follows:

> 1. My soul is a thinking thing, but it is finite, and thus can't be a thinking substance, since every substance is infinite. (IP8)

I put this in the first person singular ("my soul"), though Spinoza, in the passage on which I'm mainly drawing (KV II, Pref, 1 / 51 / 16), uses the first person plural ("our soul"). But I see no need to beg what for Descartes would be a serious question, the existence of a plurality of human minds. I think Spinoza is prepared to take the existence of that plurality for granted because he does not take Cartesian skepticism seriously. So EIIA2 boldly asserts that *man* thinks, not merely that *I* think. The NS paraphrases that by saying: "We know that we think."[20] But Spinoza's argument will proceed equally well if we accommodate Descartes on this point.

What is important for Spinoza is that the Cartesian claim that I (= my soul) am a thinking thing, when conjoined with one of the central claims of Part I (that every substance is infinite), leads quickly, by doctrines common to Descartes and

Spinoza, to the Spinozistic doctrine that my mind is a mode of thought:

> 2. Since everything which exists must be either a substance or a mode (common ground), and my soul cannot be a substance (by 1), it must be a mode of thought. There is, then, at least one mode of thought.

Now any good Cartesian would certainly agree that

> 3. If there is a mode of thought, there must be a thinking substance.

The next step, however, again invokes key results from Part 1:

> 4. There must be a thinking substance (by 2 and 3), and since there is only one substance, God (1P14), God is a thinking substance.

This amounts to an alternate demonstration of IIP1.[21] Similarly, since we are aware that a certain body (viz. our own body) is affected in many ways (IIA4), we know that

> 5. There are modes of extension.

But since modes of extension imply an extended substance, and since God is the only substance,

> 6. God is an extended substance.

Perhaps the most interesting point here is the casualness with which the assumption that there are modes of extension makes its way into the argument. If Spinoza had spelled out the demonstration of IIP2, he would have had to make that step explicit. He didn't spell out the demonstration, but I contend that if he had done so fully, he would have invoked IIA4.[22] This is to say that he tacitly takes our bodily sensations[23] to be veridical, at least to the extent that they establish the existence of modes of extension. Like skepticism about the existence of other minds, skepticism about the existence of my body is also not taken seriously.

7. As a substance, God must be infinite and perfect.

Descartes will certainly agree that God is an infinite and perfect substance. Now the parallelist conclusion comes swiftly:

8. Since God is an infinite and perfect thinking substance (4, 7), it must have an idea of each existing mode of extension. And if it is perfect, it cannot have the idea of a mode of extension, if no such mode exists.

This is a version of the traditional doctrine of God's omniscience.[24] There can be no gaps in God's knowledge; there can be no errors in his judgments. But

9. Since every mode of extension or of thought must exist in a substance (common ground), and there is only one substance (IP14 again), every mode of extension or of thought is a mode of the one substance.

We can conclude that

10. In God, the one thinking substance, there is a one-to-one correspondence between that substance's modes of extension and those ideas which have a mode of extension for their object (from 8 and 9).

This, I suggest, is Spinoza's fundamental argument for the doctrine of parallelism.[25]

7. BEYOND PARALLELISM

Let's suppose that the doctrine of parallelism is established. Parallelism is not enough. Spinoza does not hold merely that there is a one-to-one correspondence between modes of thought and modes of extension; he holds that there is an identity between them. One of the best Spinoza commentators calls this doctrine "astonishing,"[26] and so I suppose it is. Nevertheless, I think we now have the materials at hand to see why Spinoza might have taken this further step.

What is the relationship between the mode of thought and its corresponding mode of extension? Can they really be distinct from one another? At one stage of his thought, I imagine that Spinoza would have answered "yes" to this question. At any rate, in one of his earliest works[27] he does say that the soul and its object are really distinct from one another. And you can see why he might be inclined to say that. "The object," he says, "has nothing of thought." This seems a way of putting one part of the Cartesian argument for real distinction. We can conceive of a body as an extended thing, having properties which presuppose extension, such as size, shape, and motion. But none of those properties in any way involves thought, and the analysis of our concept of body does not require us to ascribe to it any further properties which would involve thought. Similarly, we can conceive the mind as a thinking thing, having properties which presuppose thought, having particular ideas and desires, but not having any properties which presuppose extension. This is shown by the Cartesian discovery that we can conceive of ourselves as minds existing in a world in which there are no bodies at all, a world in which there is nothing but us and an Evil Spirit bent on deceiving us, a spirit capable of conjuring up for us the illusion that there is a world of extended objects. Acceptance of this Cartesian doctrine would preclude the straightforward kind of materialism we find in Hobbes, for whom such mental processes as sensation and imagination are simply internal motions within the body (cf. *Lev* i, 4, ii, 2).

But if the argument for parallelism is correct, the mode of thought and its corresponding mode of extension cannot be really distinct from each other—not if that implies, as it will for an orthodox Cartesian, that the mode of thought and the mode of extension are each capable of existing without the other. Within the one substance, there *must* be a mode of thought for every mode of extension; and for every mode of thought which has a mode of extension for its object there *must* be a mode of extension. So in that same early work from which we quoted in the preceding paragraph, but in a passage which *may* date from a later stage in Spinoza's development, Spinoza writes:

> Between the idea and the object, there must necessarily be a union, because the one cannot exist without the other. For there is no thing of which there is not an idea in the thinking thing, and no idea can exist unless the thing also exists.[28]

Spinoza's concept of the union between the idea and its object here excludes the possibility of their being really distinct from one another. The idea cannot exist without its object, nor the object without its idea. Spinoza does not yet affirm the identity of the idea with its object, as he will in the *Ethics*. But Spinoza's mature affirmations of identity, affirmations conspicuous by their absence in his earlier works, are always qualified in a way which seems intended to give recognition to the Cartesian insights which had originally led him to agree with Descartes that the mind and the body are really distinct: "a mode of extension and the idea of that mode are one and the same thing, *but expressed in two ways . . .*" (IIP7S); "the mind and the body are one and the same individual, *which is conceived now under the attribute of thought, now under the attribute of extension*" (IIP21S).[29] There is a conceptual distinction between mind and body. The concept of the one does not involve the concept of the other. So conceptual analysis of the attributes of thought and extension will not reveal the necessity of a correspondence between the modes of the one attribute and

those of the other. What reveals the necessity of that correspondence, i.e., the identity of the modes, is an argument
based on the concept of God as a supremely perfect being.

8. A BUDGET OF PARADOXES

In the scholium to IIP1IC Spinoza shows that, no matter how
compelling he thinks his arguments to that point ought to be,
he expects them to encounter resistance:

> Here, no doubt, my readers will come to a halt, and think
> of many things which will give them pause. For this rea
> son I ask them to continue on with me slowly, step by
> step, and to make no judgment on these matters until they
> have read through them all. (II / 95 / 7)

What claim did Spinoza think his readers would find so disconcerting that they would be bound to raise objection to it?
The corollary to P11 reads: "The human mind is part of the
infinite intellect of God." What exactly is it which Spinoza expects to generate resistance in his readers? P11C is, indeed, a
stunning conclusion for Spinoza to reach, all the more so since
he holds that it follows without further argument from his theory of the nature of the human mind, viz. that its essence consists in its being the idea which exists in God of that mode of
extension which constitutes the human body.[30] But is it the
prima facie implausibility of this conclusion which is the problem? Or is it the fact that P11C has further consequences
which Spinoza expects his reader to find even harder to accept?

I don't know how to answer these questions, but I do know
that in the immediate vicinity of P11C Spinoza asserts two further paradoxes, closely associated with P11 and its corollary,
and certainly apt to give his readers pause. P12 informs us that

> Whatever happens in the object of the idea constituting
> the human mind must be perceived by the human mind,
> i.e., there will necessarily be an idea of that thing in the
> mind . . .

Since the object of the idea constituting the human mind is the
human body (as we learn in P13), this implies that the human
mind has at least some awareness of everything which is going
on in its body. It is not obvious why this does not amount to
an assertion that the human mind has, with respect to its own
body, an omniscience analogous to the omniscience God has
in relation to the universe as a whole. If it does amount to such
an assertion, it is certainly a lot to ask the reader to swallow.
On the face of it, there are a great many things which happen
in my body which I don't know about. If there weren't, my
doctor's work would be much easier than it is.

Again, in the scholium to P13 Spinoza observes that

> The things we have shown so far are completely general
> and do not pertain more to man than to other individuals,
> all of which, though in different degrees, are nevertheless
> animate. For of each thing there is necessarily an idea in
> God, of which God is the cause in the same way as he is
> of the idea of the human body . . . (II / 96 / 26)

The word here translated by "animate" (*animata*) is simply an
adjectival form of the Latin word for soul (*anima*), so it would
be reasonable to read this as saying that, in the same sense in
which man has a soul, all things have a soul.[31] I take it that
this is a doctrine which would be as obnoxious to Cartesian
common sense as the hypothesis of Roberval we alluded to in
§3.

What are we to make of these paradoxes? Once I tried to
deal with the problem of the mind's apparent omniscience
with respect to the states of its own body by suggesting that

minds may perceive all the states of their own bodies, but will not be conscious of their perceptions unless they contain, in addition to the ideas of modes of extension, ideas of those ideas.[32] This still seems to me to be strongly suggested by IIP23. But it looks as though that won't do. Arguably,[33] IIPP20-22 imply that each mind will contain an idea of each of its ideas, so that if consciousness is constituted by the mind's containing an idea of one of its ideas, the mind ought to be conscious of all the states of its body.[34]

Now I'm more inclined to think that if you asked Spinoza whether P12 implies that the mind is omniscient with respect to the states of its own body, he would remind you that he does not think that either the mind's knowledge of the parts of its body (P24) or its knowledge of itself (P29) is at all adequate. My awareness of what is going on in my body is usually highly confused.[35] This implies, I take it, that if I were to try to express my awareness of my body linguistically, I would not be able to do so in a way that would accurately reflect the nature of my body, or at least would not be able to do so simply on the basis of that immediate awareness. If we think of P12 as part of a theory of the mind generated by the intuitions Descartes was struggling to express when he talked about the mind's "substantial union" with the body, this will not seem at all unreasonable. The tack on which I step penetrates my skin and I feel pain. The sensation of pain, on Spinoza's theory, is an awareness of the damage just done to my body. But I am not naturally inclined to articulate my awareness of that damage in those terms. Only with the help of collateral information can I interpret that sensation as having the kind of object it has.

What of the claim that all things are animate? Partly, I think, this must be simply a deduction from preceding propositions. If there must be in God an idea of every thing that exists (P3), and if, in the case of human beings, that idea constitutes the soul of the thing (P11), then we would need some reason to deny that other things have a soul. And it's not clear what that reason would be. Partly, I think, it is a claim Spinoza finds plausible because of the connection between the concept of the soul and the concept of life. The Latin word for soul, *anima*, can also mean wind, air, or breath. Since breathing is one of the characteristic manifestations of life, it is understandable that one classical meaning of *anima* should be: the principle of life. Now I believe Spinoza does really think it appropriate to conceive of all things as living. At any rate, when he defines *life*, he defines it as *the force through which things persevere in their being*.[36] And that force is certainly something he would ascribe to all things (E IIIP6). To the extent that all things are, in that sense, alive, they all have a soul. But this does not, of course, mean that the 'souls' of very simple bodies engage in anything like a human mental life. The reasons for this will appear in our next section, but it is already implicit in the qualification Spinoza attaches to this paradox: all things are animate, but in different degrees.[37]

9. A DUALIST IN SPITE OF HIMSELF?

Some scholars have felt that, in spite of Spinoza's affirmation of the identity of mind and body, his affinities are far more with dualism than with materialism.[38] Consider the following line of thought. Spinoza tells us that the extended substance and the thinking substance are one and the same substance. But he also tells us that the attributes of these substances can be conceived as being really distinct from each other, which is to say that each can be understood without the aid of the other (E IP10). He tells us that the mind and the body are one and the same thing, conceived now under the attribute of thought, now under the attribute of extension. But he also tells us that the modes of these attributes must be understood through the attributes of which they are modes, and not through any other (IIP6). This is to say that an account of the mind, say, as a mode of thought, must be entirely in terms of the attribute of thought. In no sense can we explain the mind by appealing to features of the body. And conversely, an explanation of the features of a mode of extension, say, a human body, must be entirely in terms of the features of other bodies. In no sense can we explain the body by appealing to features of the mind. Not only can there be no causal interaction between mind and body, but each is inherently irreducible to the other. If this is so, then Spinoza's professed monism is merely verbal. With respect to the two attributes we know, and putting aside those which we do not know, Spinoza is as dualistic as Descartes.

Scholars for whom I otherwise have the greatest respect think this, and yet it seems to me profoundly mistaken. For me the true affinities of Spinoza's theory of the relation between mind and body are with materialism. And here I would appeal to the exegetical principle I alluded to in my introduction: if we would understand what Spinoza means by saying that the mind and the body are one and the same thing, conceived under different attributes, then we must see what consequences Spinoza thinks follow from this. If we do, I think we will find that subsequent materialists had reason to see a precursor in Spinoza.

IO. SPINOZA'S MATERIALISM

Spinoza begins his account of the human mind in PII, when he says that the first thing which constitutes the actual being of the human mind is the idea of some thing which actually exists. This sounds quite an innocent proposition, but if we reflect on it, we find that it has some surprising implications. For one thing, it implies that it is of the essence of the human mind to be related to something else, specifically, something else which exists. Insofar as the mind is characterized as an idea, Spinoza also implies something about the nature of the relationship. For an idea, in the technical language which Spinoza inherits from Descartes, is a representation of the thing of which it is the idea. In the Cartesian usage, nothing is normally presumed about the existence of the object of the idea. I may perfectly well have an idea of a golden mountain without there being a golden mountain. It is only in the case of God that my possession of an idea implies the actual existence of a thing corresponding to my idea. But in Spinoza, the idea which first constitutes the actual being of my mind must be an idea of something existing. In P11, Spinoza does not say *what* the idea which is my mind must be the idea of. But by P13 he has told us that the object of the idea constituting my mind must be the body. If we put these two propositions together, we may conclude that it is essential to the human mind to be a representation of an actually existing human body.[39] The mind cannot exist apart from the human body. Its essence is to be an idea of that existing body. If we conceive of it as being capable of existing apart, we must be conceiving of it inadequately. So the existence of the mind is tied, in the most intimate way possible, to the existence of the body.

In the scholium to P13, Spinoza remarks that from these propositions we understand not only that the human mind is united to the body, but also what the union of the mind and body is. This scholium sets a theme for the remainder of Part II, and indeed for most of the remainder of the *Ethics*. If we are to understand the nature of any mind, we must understand the nature of the object to which it is necessarily related. If we are to understand what distinguishes the human mind from the other minds which our metaphysic tells us must exist,

> it is necessary for us to know the nature of its object . . .
> that is, the human body . . .

Spinoza begs off from a detailed examination of the differences between human bodies and other bodies, and contents himself here with the general statement that

> the more a body surpasses others in its capacity to do many things at once, and to be acted on by many other bodies at once, the more its mind surpasses others in its capacity to perceive many things at once; the more the actions of a body depend on itself alone, and the less other bodies concur with it in acting [i.e., the less it requires the concurrence of other bodies to do what it does], the more its mind will be capable of understanding things distinctly.

This scholium sets a program for the remainder of Part II. Immediately after it, we encounter an excursus into physics, an attempt to state certain general principles common to all bodies, what I would identify as the fundamental laws which explicate the nature of extension, and an attempt to derive certain subordinate laws of nature from those fundamental laws. In the preceding chapter I suggested that this passage has a certain interest in its own right, as illustrating how the attribute of extension is related to its infinite modes. But Spinoza's justification for introducing it here is that he needs to explain at least this much about the nature of bodies if he is to demonstrate the things he wishes to demonstrate about the human mind, its capacities for knowledge, and the limitations on those capacities.

He wishes to introduce us to the notion of a composite body, which will be capable of being acted on in many ways by other bodies, without losing its own identity. With the simplest bodies, identity is secured, unproblematically, Spinoza seems to think, by their motion and rest.[40] But bodies vary enormously in their complexity: composite bodies of the first degree of complexity may be composed only of the simplest possible bodies; but the degrees of complexity range to infinity, and the human body is extremely complex. This gives it the capacity to affect other bodies in a wide variety of ways, but also the capacity to be affected by other bodies in a wide variety of ways. These various capacities of the human body to affect and be affected are rigorously correlated with the capacities of the human mind to know.[41]

What the human mind knows, in the first instance, is its own body. It is, in the first instance, the idea of its body. Insofar as the human body is a highly complex individual, so the mind is a highly complex idea, with a degree of complexity matching that in the body. It must, as we have seen, contain an idea of everything that happens in the human body (P12). This, as we've noted, is a highly paradoxical proposition, but what Spinoza wishes chiefly to emphasize is that the mind's knowledge of other things—its knowledge of bodies other than its own in sense perception (P16), its memory of the past (P18), its knowledge of itself (PP20-23), its knowledge of the common properties of all material objects (PP37-39), even its knowledge of the essence of God (PP45-47)—all of these depend on the fact that it first has knowledge of its own body. Indeed, the same dependence holds of mental functions which we might not wish to describe as knowledge of other things. So imagination (P17), too, is explained as a function of the mind's knowledge of the states of its own body.[42] It is hard to see how any philosopher could give a greater priority to knowledge of the body than Spinoza has.

And just as the knowledge that we have is explained in terms of the mind's awareness of its own body, so are the limitations of that knowledge. If the mind's knowledge of external bodies (PP25,26), and of itself (P29), is inadequate and confused, this is fundamentally because its knowledge of the parts of its own body is inadequate and confused (P24). For its knowledge of other things is mediated through that bodily awareness.

Earlier I said that if we followed out the consequences of Spinoza's identification of the mind with the body, we would see that its fundamental thrust is materialistic rather than dualistic. It is true that some of the general propositions Spinoza enunciates early in Part II have a dualistic ring to them. Spinoza's denial of interaction, his insistence that modes of one attribute must have only other modes of that attribute as their cause, goes way beyond anything Descartes maintained in his separation of the mind from the body. But if we follow out the details of Spinoza's treatment of the mind, as it develops in the course of Part II, I do not see how we can characterize it as anything but a materialistic program.[43] To understand the mind, we must understand the body, without which the mind could not function or even exist. In spite of all the parallelistic talk, the order of understanding never proceeds from mind to body.[44]

11. FREEDOM

Now there are difficulties with this reading of Spinoza, difficulties which I shall come to shortly. But first I should like to present you with one more piece of evidence in its favor. One of the most radically anti-Cartesian aspects of Spinoza's doctrine of the unity of mind and body is its implication that human freedom, in the sense of causally undetermined action, is an illusion.

In the Cartesian system, the material world is conceived as a realm in which everything which happens, happens as the result of some cause. Bodies are inherently inert in the sense that they will not undergo change of any kind unless acted on by something external to themselves. Usually that something external is another body, though sometimes, in the case of the voluntary motions of human bodies, it may be a mind. The voluntary motions of human bodies occur because some mind wills them. The mental realm is conceived as being an exception to the general reign of determinism. Although events in the mental realm may occur as the result of some cause, as, for example, when the stimulation of the body's sense organs causes the mind to perceive an external object, often they will not. The mind has the capacity to exercise a will which is free in the sense of not being determined by any causes. It exercises this capacity both in the judgments it makes and in its causation of the voluntary motions of the body. And some readers of Descartes have seen a very intimate connection between Descartes' dualism and his indeterminism. They have suggested that the dualism was largely motivated by a desire to exempt human beings from the determinism which otherwise prevails throughout nature.[45] Whether or not this is the primary motivation for Descartes' dualism, it certainly seems to me to be an important aspect of his dualism that it allows for this kind of freedom.

Spinoza, notoriously, rejects Descartes' indeterminism and criticizes Descartes for conceiving of man as a kingdom within a kingdom (see E III Pref). He insists that we should rather conceive of man as a part of nature, where that implies that we should conceive of him as being subject to the same causal laws as the rest of nature. How does he arrive at this position? His official demonstration of it, in IIP48, appeals to his denial of interaction. He deduces that the mind has no absolute or free will by appealing to the mind's status as a determinate mode of the attribute of thought, and the general proposition that all determinate modes of any attribute must be determined by prior determinate modes of that attribute in a causal sequence which extends to infinity.

But elsewhere, I think, Spinoza gives us a more accurate understanding of the process of thought by which he reached this conclusion. As I noted in chapter 1 (§1) Spinoza's first published work was an exposition of the Cartesian philosophy, an attempt, in fact, to present Descartes' *Principles* in geometric fashion. In a preface to that work, written by Lodewijk Meyer on Spinoza's instructions, Meyer cautions the reader that the opinions contained therein do not represent Spinoza's own views, that Spinoza differs from Descartes on many points. Of the many differences, Meyer instances particularly Descartes' belief that the will is endowed with a liberty of indeterminism. Our author, he says, referring to Spinoza,

> . . . does not think that the will is endowed with such liberty . . . Indeed, [he thinks that] in asserting these things . . . Descartes only assumes, but does not prove that the human mind is a substance thinking absolutely. Though our author admits, of course, that there is a thinking substance in nature, he nevertheless denies that it constitutes the essence of the human mind . . . [J]ust as the human body is not extension absolutely, but only an extension, determined in a certain way according to the laws of extended nature by motion and rest, so also the human mind, or soul, is not thought absolutely, but only a thought determined in a certain way according to the laws of thinking nature by ideas, a thought which, one infers, must exist as soon as the human body begins to exist. From this definition, he thinks, it is not difficult to demonstrate that the will is not . . . endowed with that liberty which Descartes ascribes to it. (1 / 233)

It seems to me clear from this passage that Spinoza's determinism about the mind is being inferred from essentially two premises: that determinism reigns in the physical world, and that the mind and the body, properly understood, are one and the same thing. Of course, Spinoza does not affirm the identity of mind and body here. He only affirms that the human mind begins to exist when the body begins to exist. But I think this is intended as an affirmation of the dependence of the mind on the body. In an earlier work, the *Short Treatise* (App II, §3), Spinoza had said that the soul or mind had its origin in the body. I think that is also his view in the *Ethics*. Part II is subtitled: "Of the Nature and Origin of the Mind." If we ask what the origin of the mind is according to Part II, the answer seems to be that it is an idea arising in the thinking thing as a result of the fact that the body comes to exist in the extended thing. The first thing which constitutes the actual being of the mind is that it is the idea of an actually existing body (IIPP11, 13).

We see a good illustration of the connection between materialism and determinism early in Part III of the *Ethics*. In IIIP2 Spinoza applies the denial of interaction previously announced in IIP6 to the special case of the (human) mind and body:

> The body cannot determine the mind to thinking, and the mind cannot determine the body to motion, to rest, or to anything else (if there is anything else).

In the scholium he undertakes to reply to the objections of those who are persuaded that the body does a great many things at the mind's command. One of the objections is that human beings do many things which depend on free (i.e., uncaused) decisions of the mind (II / 142 / 23). The objection seems to assume that these interventions will not be intelligible unless the mind is insulated from the causal processes of the physical world, and that Spinoza's theory of the relation between mind and body makes no provision for that insulation.

Spinoza's reply sounds a very familiar theme: men believe themselves free only because they are aware of their actions and not aware of the causes by which their actions are determined. Really they are no more free than the drunkard, who believes that he speaks freely the things he later, when sober, wishes he had not said. But in this context he gives that familiar answer a special twist:

> the decisions of the mind are nothing but the appetites themselves, which therefore vary as the disposition of the body varies. For each one governs everything from his affect; those who are torn by contrary affects do not know what they want, and those who are not moved by any affect are very easily driven here and there.
>
> All these things, indeed, show clearly that the decision of the mind and the appetite and determination of the body by nature exist together—or rather, are one and the same thing, which we call a decision when it is considered under, and explained through the attribute of thought, and which we call a determination when it is considered under the attribute of extension and deduced from the laws of motion and rest. (II / 143 / 33-144 / 8)

This neatly turns the objection around. Freedom is an illusion. A theory of the mind-body relation which allowed for it would be making provision for an illusion. What is required instead is a theory which recognizes determinism and explains why it obtains at the mental level as well as at the physical level. The theory that modes of thought and modes of extension must exist together—or rather, that because these modes *must* exist together, mind and body are one and the same thing, considered in two different ways—does just that.

I conclude, then, that if we look to the further development of Spinoza's doctrine of mind-body identity in Parts II and III of the *Ethics*, if we look to the consequences which he thinks follow from his doctrine that the mind and the body are one and the same thing, conceived in two different ways, we shall find that the fundamental thrust of Spinoza's system is anti-dualistic, that it is a form of materialistic monism.

12. THE ETERNITY OF THE MIND

Earlier I remarked that there are difficulties in the reading of
Spinoza that I have been offering, and I promised to address
them shortly. The time to do so has now come. What I have
in mind most particularly is Spinoza's doctrine of the eternity
of the mind, outlined toward the end of Part v of the *Ethics*.
Spinoza tells us that

> the human mind cannot be absolutely destroyed with the
> body but something of it remains which is eternal. (P23)

The eternal portion of the mind is

> an idea which expresses the essence of the human body,
> *sub specie aeternitatis*, and which pertains to the essence
> of the human mind. (P23S)

Insofar as the mind possesses this knowledge of the essence of
the human body *sub specie aeternitatis*, it knows God and itself through the third kind of knowledge (PP30-31), and de-
lighting in that knowledge (P32), loves God with an eternal
love (P33), free of all passive affects (P24).

This doctrine is one of the most difficult things to understand in all of Spinoza. But however obscure it may be, it does
at least seem to cast doubt on the interpretation I have been
presenting. How, if the mind and the body are one and the
same thing, conceived in different ways, can a part of the mind
survive the destruction of the body? How, if it is essential to
the mind to be the idea of an actually existing body, can something of it remain which is eternal? We have been proceeding
on the exegetical principle that the meaning of Spinoza's metaphysical formulas is at least partly determined by the consequences he thinks he can derive from them. We learn what
Spinoza means in proclaiming the identity of the mind and the
body by examining the context in which this doctrine is

embedded. And in Part v we learn that the context contains affirmations which sound, in many ways, very like a traditional theory of the immortality of the soul. To that extent, Spinoza seems to be conceiving the relation of mind and body dualistically. If the mind can exist apart from the body, as these last propositions of the *Ethics* seem to say,[46] how can it not be really distinct from the body? Do not these pages strongly confirm that interpretation which makes a dualist of Spinoza?

In responding to this objection, I think I had best begin by confessing candidly that in spite of many years of study, I still do not feel that I understand this part of the *Ethics* at all adequately. I feel the freedom to confess that, of course, because I also believe that no one else understands it adequately either. But I do think I understand enough of Spinoza's doctrine to make the following observations:

1. If the doctrine of the eternity of the mind presents a difficulty for my interpretation it must also present a difficulty for dualistic interpretations of Spinoza. For whatever we make of the claim that mind and body are one, we all agree that Spinoza commits himself to a thoroughgoing parallelism, that he is committed to holding that for every mode of extension, there is a corresponding mode of thought, and conversely,[47] and that the relations between the modes of thought parallel those between the modes of extension. Insofar as the doctrine of the eternity of the mind suggests that there can be a mind (or a part of a mind) without a corresponding body, it threatens to contradict the parallelism which every interpreter agrees is a fundamental part of Spinoza's system.

2. But I am not yet convinced that Spinoza's doctrine of the eternity of (a part of) the mind does imply a violation of parallelism. So far as I can see, the key to understanding the doctrine of the eternity of the mind must lie in a proper understanding of IIP8 and its corollary and scholium. P8 says:

The ideas of non-existent modes must be contained in the infinite idea of God in the same way that the formal essences of the modes are contained in the attributes of God.

Now it is, at the very best, not immediately clear what this means, and I am not going to attempt a thorough explanation of it here. But this much does seem tolerably clear: first, that the ideas spoken of here do have an object (the "formal essence" of the singular thing), even if that object is not a mode which can be said to exist at a particular time; and second, whatever the manner in which the object of these ideas exists, so the ideas exist also.[48] If the objects do not exist at a particular time, then neither do the ideas. So I do not think Spinoza's doctrine does imply that the mind or a part of the mind can exist apart from the body in any sense in which existence would imply having any temporal properties (such as existing *after the body dies*). Insofar as Spinoza uses language which suggests something different—as at the end of P20S, when he writes that "it is time now to pass to those things which pertain to the mind's duration without relation to the body"—I think he is trying to accommodate popular views within his system in a way the system will not really allow.

3. But although there is a certain attempt at accommodation in the latter part of Part V, I think this must have been motivated by a conviction that popular views about immortality are confused attempts to express something true (cf. P23S, P34S), not by a desire to make his system more palatable to the orthodox. Otherwise he would not go to such pains to emphasize the differences between *his* doctrine of the eternity of the mind and traditional conceptions of immortality. Spinoza does not have a doctrine of personal immortality. What 'remains' after the destruction of the body is not a person. For Spinoza says that the capacity for imagination and memory

exists only so long as the body exists (VP21), and he regards continuity of memory as essential to the continuity of the person. This appears in his discussion of the case of the Spanish poet who suffered so from amnesia that he forgot his past life entirely and would not believe that the comedies and tragedies he had written were his own (IVP39S). Spinoza remarks that it would be difficult to say of such a man that he was the same man. In this he anticipates Locke's doctrine that personality cannot survive radical disruptions of consciousness. What I cannot be aware of as my own past actions *are* not my own past actions, even though they may have been performed by a body physically continuous with this body.

If, as I have argued, Spinoza's position has affinities with materialism, it is not a simple-minded materialism. The person is not simply identical with a body, but rather is identical with a body functioning at a certain level of performance, engaging in sophisticated cognitive activities which require a complex physiological basis. Neither is Spinoza's final position one which Descartes would find congenial. If memory does not survive the destruction of the body, then *I* do not survive the destruction of the body. For some memory of my past actions is essential to my being the person who performed them. So Spinoza's doctrine of the eternity of the mind cannot offer the kind of consolation provided by its analogue in Descartes. Whatever the doctrine of the eternity of the mind does mean, it does not mean that *I* can entertain any hope of immortality.

III
&

On Man's Well-Being

I. FROM DESCARTES TO HOBBES TO SPINOZA

IN THIS FINAL chapter I turn to Spinoza's psychology and moral philosophy, as expounded in Parts III through V of the *Ethics*. The central doctrine which unifies all these topics, which provides Spinoza with a foundation, both for his psychology and for his moral philosophy, is the doctrine of the *conatus*, the striving for self-preservation which Spinoza sees as animating all of nature. I want to show how he understood this doctrine, why he held it, and what work it did for him in the *Ethics*. As before, I shall emphasize Spinoza's relationship to Descartes, whom Spinoza singles out for criticism by name, both in the Preface to Part III and in the Preface to Part V. Such explicit mention of an opponent is rare in Spinoza.

The further we get into the latter parts of the *Ethics*, however, the more important other influences become. In this chapter Hobbes will have a strong claim on our attention. My contention is that Descartes' unsatisfactory and programmatic ventures in this area posed problems for Spinoza, problems to which he found some solution in Hobbes. But what Spinoza found in Hobbes he transformed radically. Hobbes' famous remark about Spinoza—that Spinoza had "cut through him a bar's length, for he durst not write so boldly"—was prompted, not by the *Ethics*, but by the *Theologico-Political Treatise*.¹ But if the argument of this chapter is correct, the remark would have been equally appropriate to the *Ethics*.

2. CLIMBING THE TREE OF PHILOSOPHY

We begin with Descartes. In the first chapter I alluded to his comparison of philosophy to a tree, whose roots are metaphysics, whose trunk is physics, and whose branches are all the other sciences, the most important of which is moral philosophy. Descartes never managed a complete presentation of his philosophical system. The nearest he came was in the *Principles*, which gives us the roots and trunk of the tree, but is, by Descartes' own admission, incomplete, in that it does not give us the botany, zoology, and anthropology which were to prepare the way for medicine and morals (cf. *Principles* IV, 188). In his later correspondence, however, and in the *Passions of the Soul* Descartes does leap over the missing parts to give us a general idea of the lines he would have taken in a fully systematic presentation of his moral philosophy.[2]

Descartes was led to develop this aspect of his philosophy, out of its logical order, mainly by his correspondence with Princess Elisabeth, who suffered from chronic depression and hoped that the philosopher would be able to give her some relief from her melancholy. Descartes began by recommending that they study together Seneca's *De vita beata*, a title we might translate *On the Happy Life*.[3] Though Descartes had recommended this book without having read it recently, and found Seneca's way of treating his topic unsatisfactory when he did reread it, it was evidently not just the Stoic philosopher's reputation which led Descartes to propose his work for discussion. Descartes did have a strong sympathy with Seneca's outlook. He agreed with Seneca's starting point: all men want to live happily, and the problem is to see what will make your life happy (K 164). Moreover, he understood the goal of happiness in a very Stoic way: it consists in a life of perfect contentment of mind and interior satisfaction. He thought that the wise man, using his reason, could attain this peace of mind:

> True philosophy . . . teaches that, even amid the saddest disasters and most bitter pains, a man can always be content, provided that he knows how to use his reason.[4]

What a man must do, to achieve this contentment, is to limit his desires for things which nature or fortune may have placed beyond his grasp (K 165). So the fundamental task of the moral philosopher is to teach the control of passions by reason:

> The true use of our reason in the conduct of life consists only in examining and considering without passion the value of all the mental and physical perfections which can be acquired by our conduct, so that—since ordinarily we must give up some to have others—we should always choose the best.

Not that Descartes thinks we should live without passion:

> I am not of the opinion that we must entirely scorn the passions, nor that we should try to exempt ourselves from having them. It is enough that we should render them subject to reason. (K 170)

This project of controlling the passions by reason led Elisabeth to ask for a definition of the passions, so that they might be well known. "Those," she wrote, "who name them perturbations of the soul would persuade me that their force consists only in dazzling and mastering reason, had not experience shown me that there are some which carry us to reasonable actions."[5] Descartes responded by producing his last major work, *The Passions of the Soul*.

89

3. THE CARTESIAN THEORY OF THE PASSIONS

Descartes began his work with the bold claim that nothing shows better the defectiveness of the sciences of the ancients than what they have written about the passions.[6] What does Descartes think is the most important defect in ancient psychology? He does not say, but I suggest we take him to be thinking of the Platonic doctrine, accepted with some modification in the Aristotelian tradition, that the soul is divided into distinct parts capable of coming into conflict. Since Descartes makes the simplicity and indivisibility of the soul or mind one of the key distinctions between mind and body (AT VII, 85-86), he cannot allow any such division. According to Descartes, the struggles philosophers have customarily imagined between an inferior, sensing part of the soul and a superior, reasoning part of the soul, or between natural appetites and a will conceived as rational appetite, must be reinterpreted as conflicts between mind and body:

> For in us there is only one soul and this soul has in itself no diversity of parts. The same soul which is sensitive is reasonable, and all its appetites are volitions. (§47)

Our tendency to think of the soul as if it consisted of different persons with contrary impulses comes, according to Descartes, from our having failed to adequately distinguish the soul's functions from those of the body and from our not having understood the mechanism of mind-body interaction.

4. THE PINEAL GLAND AND CONFLICT

Although the soul, being indivisible, is united to all the parts of the body together (§30), there is a small gland in the brain in which it exercises its functions more particularly than in any other part of the body, the pineal gland (§31). The pineal gland is the locus of interaction between the soul and the so-called "animal spirits," a subtle fluid generated by the heating of the blood in the heart and pumped through the nervous system to act as an intermediary between the stimulation of our sense organs and the mind in sensation, and between our mind and our muscles in voluntary bodily movements (§§7-8). When the mind wishes to move the body, it imparts a certain motion to the pineal gland, which in turn imparts a motion to the animal spirits, which enter the appropriate muscles, causing some to tighten and contract, and others to relax and expand (§11). Of course, the soul does not directly will any particular movement of the pineal gland. It wills, say, to move the body's legs. Fortunately, "nature" has joined the motion of the pineal gland necessary to produce that effect to that particular volition (§44). A similar process, beginning in the nerve endings and ending in the pineal gland, is integral to sensation (§§12-13).

Spinoza's mockery of this hypothesis in the Preface to Part V set the tone for much subsequent discussion. And certainly if it is a requirement of reason that a cause have something in common with its effect (1P3), if there is a conceptual problem in understanding how an immaterial substance could cause a material one to move, it is not solved by postulating that the material thing is very easy to move. But Descartes has reasons for his hypothesis which are not entirely discreditable. He thinks there must be some one organ in which the various impressions coming through our senses are united. All of our exterior sense organs are double, and yet we have, as he puts it, one simple thought of one thing at the same time. The pineal gland's mediation is supposed to explain how that is possible (§32).

What Platonists might be inclined to call psychological conflict is the result of contrary actions on the pineal gland, which is moved in one way by the soul and in another by the animal spirits. Some motions of the animal spirits, of course, merely cause the pineal gland to represent to the soul the external objects which have affected our sense organs. But others generate passions which may cause in the soul a desire for something it would otherwise choose to flee:

> What principally makes this conflict appear is that, because the will does not have the power to excite the passions directly, it is constrained to . . . apply itself to considering successively different things, some of which may happen to have the force to change the course of the spirits for a moment, while others may not, with the result that the spirits may immediately resume their course . . . So the soul feels itself pushed, almost at the same time, to desire and not to desire one and the same thing. (§47)

Descartes is evidently denying here the possibility of the soul's desiring and not desiring the same thing at precisely the same time, a position which seems to justify the doubts of some commentators as to whether Descartes has understood the profundity of Platonic psychology, but one to which Descartes evidently feels forced by his doctrine that the soul is a simple substance.[7] The need to exclude all conflict with reason from the soul no doubt explains (partially, at least) why Descartes defines passions of the soul as "perceptions, or sensations, or emotions of the soul, which one relates particularly to it, and which are caused, preserved and strengthened by some movement of the [animal] spirits" (§27).

5. CLASSIFYING THE PASSIONS

If the claim that the soul is a simple, indivisible substance helps to motivate Descartes' definition of the passions and his understanding of psychological conflict, it also influences his classification of the passions. On Descartes' analysis there are six simple and primitive passions: wonder, love, hate, desire, joy and sadness. To call these passions simple and primitive is not to say that they are indefinable. Descartes offers definitions of each of them. But none of them can be explained in terms of any of the others; together they form a sufficient basis for explaining all the other passions—esteem and scorn, pride and humility, hope and fear, courage and cowardice, and so on—all of which can be shown to be species of the basic six. Descartes takes particular pride in this project of classification. Having given a preliminary sketch of his analysis in §§53-67, he writes:

> That is the order which seems to me best for enumerating the passions. In following it, I know that I separate myself from all those who have previously written on the passions,[8] but I do not do this without good reason. For they draw their enumeration from the fact that they distinguish in the sensitive part of the soul two appetites, which they call concupiscible and irascible.[9] But because, as I have said before, I do not recognize any distinction of parts in the soul, that seems to me to mean only that the soul has two faculties, one of desiring and the other of getting angry. And because it has in the same way faculties of wondering, loving, hoping, fearing, [etc.] . . . I do not see why they wanted to relate all of them to concupiscence and anger. (§68)

Descartes' point, I take it, is that if, to explain the phenomena of conflicting desires, we postulate parts of the soul, there is no reason to limit those parts to just two or three.

6. TREATING THE PASSIONS *EN PHYSICIEN*

In a prefatory letter to the *Passions of the Soul* Descartes writes that his design in that work was to explain the passions, not as an orator might, nor even as a moral philosopher might, but only "en physicien" (AT XI, 326). We might translate this as CSM does: "as a natural philosopher." Or having regard to the character of the work Descartes wrote, we might prefer "as a physiologist," since he begins by giving the most detailed discussion of human physiology he published in his lifetime, explaining the mechanics of voluntary movement, the perception of external objects, and bodily sensation, as well as the passions which are his primary subject. Not only does he define his fundamental passions in terms of the motions of the animal spirits which cause them (§§79-92), but he devotes a good deal of space (§§97-135) to detailing the physiological accompaniments of the passions, as a way of confirming empirically the correctness of his causal theory. Still, we might argue with equal force for simply rendering *physicien* by *physician*, since Descartes is as much concerned to provide a remedy for the passions as he is to understand their physiology.

He does not think the passions are necessarily evil. One key difference between Descartes and the Stoics, to whom he often seems to owe so much, is that he maintains that the passions are all good in their nature, and that we have nothing to avoid in them but their misuse:[10] "I cannot persuade myself that nature has given men any passion which is always vicious and has no use which is good and praiseworthy" (§175). Indeed, Descartes will conclude his work (§212) with the thought that the greatest sweetness experienced in this life is felt by those who are most moved by the passions.[11] He admits it may not always be easy to see what the use of a passion is, but in general the utility of the passions consists in that they dispose the soul to will the things nature tells us are useful to us (§52).

Descartes explains this notion of something's being useful to us in two ways. Insofar as the soul is thought of in relation to the body, "the natural use [of the passions] is to move the soul to consent and contribute to actions which can help to

preserve the body or to render it in some way more perfect"
(§137). From that point of view, sadness and hate are even
more necessary than joy and love, since it is more important
to reject things which harm the body than to acquire those
which add some perfection to the body, but which are not necessary to its continued existence (§137). On the other hand, if
we consider the soul without relation to the body, the love
which comes from a true knowledge of good is incomparably
better than the hate which comes from a true knowledge of
evil, and cannot be excessive, since its effect is only to so unite
us with a true good that we are never disposed to put self-love
above love of the true good (§139). Hate is never so slight that
it is not harmful, since hatred of a known evil never incites us
to any action to which we would not better be led by love of
a known good (§140).

7. A REMEDY FOR THE PASSIONS

Though we have yet to speak of any remedies for the passions,
it will be clear already that Descartes' project of explaining the
passions *en physicien* does not admit any sharp separation
from a treatment of them as a moral philosopher. This en-
croachment on the territory of the moral philosopher becomes
still more evident as Descartes develops his theory of *générosité*—classed both as a passion and as a virtue, and proclaimed
to be the key to all the other virtues and a general remedy
against all the disorders of the passions (§161). *Générosité,*[12]
a term best translated into English, perhaps, by *nobility,* consists in two things: (1) knowing that nothing really pertains to
you except the free disposition of your volitions, the only legitimate grounds for praise and blame being that you have
used your free will well or ill; and (2) feeling in yourself a firm
and constant resolution to use your free will well, i.e., never

to fail to will what you judge to be best. To possess such a will is to be perfectly virtuous (§153).

Descartes' *générosité* represents an ideal of character. Descartes' noble man will esteem himself as highly as he legitimately can (§153); he will not think himself much inferior to others who surpass him in wealth, honor, knowledge, beauty, birth or any other good; neither will he think himself much superior to those whom he surpasses in those respects; for he will think all those things of little moment compared with a good will and he will recognize that others, of themselves, can possess the knowledge and feeling in which true nobility consists (§§154, 161); he will excuse others for their weaknesses, because he knows that their misdeeds proceed from lack of knowledge rather than from lack of good will (§154); he will be the master of his passions, particularly of his desires, of jealousy, of envy and of anger, because he will think that nothing is worth much except what depends on himself (§156); he will naturally be led to do great things and to do good to others at the expense of his own interest, but he will undertake nothing of which he does not judge himself capable (§156); and he will be unaffected by fortune, not changing his temper when prosperity or adversity befall him (§159). This happy condition may be attained by reflecting on what free will is and how great are the advantages of its proper use (§161).

8. PROBLEMS

Descartes cannot treat of the passions without engaging in moral philosophy, and yet he has some reason to be modest in his claims about what he has accomplished in his treatise, since it is far from being a fully worked out theory of morality, even by Descartes' own standards of rigor. In a letter to Elisabeth written some four years before the treatise was published (15 September 1645) Descartes had enumerated several truths which he thought particularly important for guiding our lives. Some of these truths do make their appearance in the treatise on the passions: that there is a God, on whom all things depend, whose perfections are infinite, whose power is immense, and whose decrees are infallible (K 171, cf. PA §145); or that the passions tend to represent the goods they incline us to pursue as being greater than they really are (K 173, cf. PA §211). Others do not: Descartes does not say in this treatise that we must have a just idea of the vast extent of God's creation, lest we think too much of this world and the life we lead in it; though he certainly implies that our soul will have a life beyond this life, in which it can enjoy a contentment greater than any it experiences here, he does not *say* that the soul is immortal, much less emphasize it, nor does he work out the theory of intellectual joy which an account of the happiness of a soul separated from its body would require.[13]

And sometimes when those useful truths of the letter to Elisabeth do make their appearance, the difficulties they involve are avoided rather than met. For example, Descartes had written to Elisabeth that

> although each of us is a person, separate from others, whose interests are consequently distinct, in some way, from those of the rest of the world, nevertheless one should remember that one cannot maintain oneself in existence alone, and that one is, in fact, one of the parts of the universe, and more particularly still, one of the parts of this earth, one of the parts of this State, of this society, of this family, to which one is joined by one's residence, or by one's oath, or by one's birth. It is necessary *always* to prefer the interests of the whole of which one is a part to those of one's own particular person. (K 172, my emphasis)

Descartes will sound this note again in his discussion of love in the treatise, where he will argue that it is a consequence of his definition of love that the lover should imagine himself to be only a part of a whole of which the thing he loves is another part (§80), that the lover will necessarily desire for what he loves the things he believes to be suitable for it (§81), and that in certain circumstances he will be prepared to sacrifice himself to the interests of the thing he loves (§83). But he is extremely vague about what those circumstances are.[14]

In the letter to Elisabeth, he had no sooner recommended always sacrificing one's own interests to those of the whole than he immediately introduced a qualification:

> Nevertheless, one should do this with measure and discretion. For one would be wrong to expose oneself to a great evil in order to secure only a small good for one's parents or one's country. And if a man is worth more, by himself, than all the rest of his city, he would be wrong to want to lose himself to save it.

When Elisabeth inquired how one might measure these matters, Descartes replied that it was difficult to do so exactly, but that fortunately it was not necessary to be very exact. "It is enough to satisfy one's conscience and in that one can make considerable allowance for one's inclinations."

9. HOBBESIAN PSYCHOLOGY

If Descartes' moral philosophy centers on the problem of the individual's control of his passions, and acknowledges, without seriously attempting to resolve, the problem of the individual's relation to the society of which he is a part, the reverse is true of Hobbes. Hobbes is certainly acutely aware of human irrationality, of the extent to which men are subservient to their passions.[15] But his central concern is not so much to help men achieve mastery over their passions as it is to persuade them of the advantages of submitting to a sovereign whose power is absolute. His stimulus came not from an encounter with a depressed princess, but from his awareness of the danger to a soon-to-be-deposed king. His first major political work, *The Elements of Law*, was written just two years before the English Civil War broke out in 1642, and his last, *Leviathan*, was published just two years after the war ended, with the beheading of Charles I, in 1649.

Hobbes' argument for the individual's subordination of his own desires to those of society at large, as represented by the king, is based on a theory of human nature which on the face of it is strongly egoistic. The central concepts of Hobbes' psychology are those of appetite and aversion. In keeping with his materialism, these concepts are given a physiological interpretation. Human beings, like all animals, are subject to two kinds of motion: vital and voluntary. The former are such internal motions as the circulation of the blood, breathing, nutrition, excretion, etc. The latter are such external movements as are involved in walking, speaking, raising an arm, etc. Sensation and imagination are forms of vital motion, the one resulting directly from the action on us of the things we see, hear, etc., the other resulting indirectly from such actions, but continuing after contact with the external object has been lost. All voluntary motion has its beginning in sense or imagination. When the effect of an external object has been to strengthen our vital motions, we feel this increase of vital motion as delight or pleasure. When it has been to weaken our vital motions, we feel that decrease as pain. An appetite is an internal beginning of a motion towards an object in which we take pleasure; an aversion, an internal beginning of motion away from an object which displeases us. All other human emotions are species of appetite and aversion.[16]

Hobbes tends to represent voluntary action as the result of a process of deliberation, conceived as a series of alternating appetites and aversions. The will, in the sense of the act of deciding to do one rather than the other of two alternatives, is simply the last appetite or aversion in this series, the one immediately preceding the bodily movement. Whatever the deficiencies of this account,[17] it has the consequence that whatever we do voluntarily, we do as the result of some desire. When we put this together with Hobbes' subjectivist definition of "good" as "the common name for all things that are desired, insofar as they are desired,"[18] we can readily deduce that whatever a man does voluntarily, he does for the sake of something he considers good. We need only add a small qualifier to get a characteristic expression of the kind of formula usually taken to commit Hobbes to an egoistic view of human psychology: "Whatsoever is voluntarily done, is done for some good to him that wills it" (*DC* ii, 8. Cf. *Lev* xiv, 8).

There has been much debate recently among Hobbes scholars as to whether such formulas are really as egoistic as they sound.[19] Arguably the position so far makes egoism a mere tautology, insofar as it does not exclude the possibility of a man's taking the good of others as the object of his desire, or even of his acting from a sense of duty. Indeed, Hobbes does seem to admit that people sometimes do act from benevolence or compassion or friendship or even because they consider themselves bound by a promise:

> The love whereby man loves man is understood in two ways, and good will appertains to both. But it is called one kind of love when we wish ourselves well, and another when we wish well to others. Therefore, a male neighbor is usually loved one way, a female another. For in loving the former, we seek his good, in loving the latter our own. (*DH* xii, 8)

This may suggest a somewhat cynical view of male / female relations, but the contrast with male / male relations would lose its point if Hobbes were not here attributing a genuine, if limited, benevolence to some relationships between men. Again,

> When the words are applied to persons, *to be just* signifies as much as to be delighted in just dealing, to study how to do righteousness, or to endeavor in all things to do that which is just; and *to be unjust* is to neglect righteous dealing, or think it is to be measured not according to my contract, but some present benefit. (*DC* iii, 5)

Hobbes seems to admit here that we can take pleasure in being in conformity with the moral law and that this can motivate us to sacrifice what we perceive to be, at least in the short term, our personal advantage.

Still, Hobbes did not get his reputation as an egoist for nothing. The passages just noted are there and are not to be denied their significance. But passages like the following are far more characteristic:[20]

> They who shall more narrowly look into the causes for which men come together, and delight in each other's company, shall easily find that this happens not because naturally it could not happen otherwise, but by accident. For if by nature one man should love another, i.e., as man, there could be no reason returned why every man should not equally love every man, as being equally man, or why he should rather frequent those whose society affords him honor or profit. We do not therefore by nature seek society for its own sake, but that we may receive some honor or profit from it; these we desire primarily, that secondarily . . . [W]hen we voluntarily contract society, in all manner of society we look after the object of the will, i.e., that which everyone of those who gather together propounds to himself for good. Now whatsoever seems good, is pleasant, and relates either to the senses or

the mind. But all the mind's pleasure is either glory (or to have a good opinion of oneself) or refers to glory in the end; the rest are sensual, or conducing to sensuality, which may be all comprehended under one word, *conveniences*. All society therefore is either for gain or for glory, i.e., not so much for love of our fellows, as for love of ourselves. (*DC* i, 2)

For brevity's sake I've omitted from this passage much of the forceful prose Hobbes uses to support his unsentimental view of the reasons why humans seek the society of their fellows, but even this passage does not flatly deny the existence of genuine benevolence. What it does suggest is that disinterested love of our fellows has a smaller role to play in the explanation of human behavior than does love of ourselves, and that if there should be a conflict between self-interest and the interests of others, most people most of the time would give preference to their own interests, or at any rate that they would do so if they personally stood to lose very much (or if others did not stand to gain much more than they would lose).[21]

10. HOBBESIAN POLITICS

This may not seem a very promising view of human nature on which to base an argument for forming a society, with all the accommodations that involves, but it is Hobbes' genius to have found a very powerful argument that this is precisely what men so motivated should do. His procedure is like that of a mathematician undertaking a proof by reduction to absurdity. He asks us to imagine what the life of man would be like without civil society, i.e., without some effective power established in the society to make rules governing the conduct of its members and to see that they are enforced. He shows very persuasively that the life of such men would be intolerable: "solitary, poor, nasty, brutish and short," as his famous phrase goes. The moral is that the first thing men so circumstanced should do is to try to change their situation, even at the cost of submitting to an absolute monarch (and Hobbes thinks that *is* the price men must pay for an enduring solution to their dilemma).

Why is the condition of man in the state of nature so miserable? Basically the argument is that no one, no matter how strong or how smart he is, no matter how moderate his desires are, will fare even tolerably well without a civil power to protect him from his neighbors. It is not necessary for Hobbes to suppose that man's egoism is such that all men are aggressive towards one another. The point is that it is enough to make all men insecure in their possessions if some men are sufficiently dissatisfied with what they have to poach on their neighbors. Even the strongest and the smartest must have times (e.g., in sleep or illness) when they are vulnerable even to the weakest and most stupid. And though those who are modest in their desires may themselves be pleased with little, they cannot be sure that they will not fall prey to the less amiable, not so long as they possess goods which others may covet. In the absence of the civil power, and in the absence of any reliable information about the intentions of their neighbors, their most rational way to protect their own interests will be the preemptive strike. Even those inclined to be peaceable will be forced by prudence to act aggressively.

So the condition of man in the state of nature is a war of all against all—not in the sense that each man is constantly fighting every other man, but that each man must stand ready at any moment to fight anyone. In these conditions, Hobbes says,

> there is no place for industry, because the fruit thereof is uncertain, and consequently, no culture of the earth; no navigation, nor use of the commodities that may be im-

ported by sea; no commodious building; no instruments of moving . . . such things as require much force; no knowledge of the face of the earth . . . no arts, no letters, no society, and which is worst of all, continual fear and danger of violent death . . . (*Lev* xiii, 9)

Hobbes grants that men may never have lived generally in such a condition, and so seems not to regard the social contract which offers a solution to this dilemma as an historical event—the point is rather to understand why it is rational for men to obey and support existing governments—but he also seems to think that men experience at least a close approximation to it when their country undergoes a civil war (*Lev* xiii, 11).

Hobbes' description of the way men would act in this hypothetical situation resolutely abstains from moral judgment. If man's natural condition is one of war, it follows, he says, that it is one in which "the notions of right and wrong, justice and injustice have no place. Where there is no common power, there is no law; where no law, no injustice" (*Lev* xiii, 13). If the state did not exist, everything would be permissible. And yet, Hobbes devotes two chapters of *Leviathan* (xiv, xv) to describing the immutable and eternal laws of nature which apply to this state of war, and which prescribe that men should strive for peace, lay down the natural right they have to all things, keep their promises, be grateful to those who have freely benefited them, strive to accommodate themselves to others, and so on. This is a paradox which needs to be understood.

The key seems to lie in Hobbes' doctrine of the primacy of the striving for self-preservation:

Every man is desirous of what is good for him, and shuns what is evil, but chiefly the chiefest of natural evils, which is death, and this he doth by a certain impulsion of nature, no less than that whereby a stone moves downward. (*DC* i, 7)

On the one hand, the necessity of this desire makes it inappropriate to criticize those who act on it. If a man does only what he thinks is required for his self-preservation, he acts permissibly (*Lev* xiii, 4). On the other hand, the urgency of the desire for self-preservation gives special force to the hypothetical imperatives which show the way out of the natural condition. It is a dictate of reason, i.e., "a theorem concerning what conduceth to the conservation and defence of themselves" (*Lev* xv, 41) that "every man ought to endeavor peace, as far as he has hope of obtaining it" (xiv, 4), or that "a man be willing, when others are so too, as far forth as for peace and defence of himself he shall think it necessary, to lay down this right to all things, and be contented with so much liberty against other men as he would allow other men against himself" (xiv, 5). If he wishes to preserve himself, he ought to take advantage of whatever opportunities his situation offers to leave the natural condition and become a member of a civil society by agreeing with others to set up a sovereign whose commands they will all obey and seek to have enforced. For his life is in constant danger so long as he is not a member of such a society. But each man does wish to preserve himself, and it is not a contingent fact that he does. So the consequents of these imperatives are not *hypothetical* in any objectionable sense of that term. They are not commands whose force we would only feel if we possessed certain desires which we might not have.

11. SPINOZA'S RESPONSE

In retrospect we can see that Hobbes is the founder of modern moral and political philosophy, much as Descartes is the founder of modern metaphysics and epistemology. Descartes does not have nearly the importance for the subsequent history of the former disciplines that Hobbes does. But when Spinoza was writing the *Ethics*, they seem to have loomed equally large. We can measure Descartes' importance for Spinoza by the attention he gives him in the Prefaces to Parts III and v of the *Ethics*, where he criticizes him for believing that man is a kingdom within a kingdom, exempt, in virtue of his free will, from the laws which govern the rest of nature; for failing to determine the nature and power of the affects or what the mind can do to moderate them; for believing man to be exempt from the laws of nature, and contending that man could exercise an absolute power over his passions; for trying to explain human affects through their first causes, but offering, in the end, a hypothesis more occult than any occult quality.

Some, but not all, of these criticisms will apply equally to Hobbes. Certainly he does not make man a kingdom within a kingdom. He sees man, as Spinoza does, as subject to the same laws which govern the rest of nature. And he does not imagine that man can exercise an absolute power over his passions. So his analysis of human behavior is as non-judgmental as Spinoza's. He shares with Spinoza the desire to treat human actions and appetites "just as if it were a question of lines, planes and bodies" (E III Pref). But his treatment of the nature of the affects is superficial compared with Spinoza's and he does not have much to say about what the mind can do to moderate them (as Spinoza implies at II / 137 / 21-25). This is an important defect in his philosophy. It is all very well to show that it is rational for men to form a society with their fellows and submit to its laws. But if you think that "the passions of men are commonly more potent than their reason" (*Lev* xix, 4), it is not clear how useful this advice will be.

The problem for Spinoza, then, was to construct an alternative theory free of these defects, a theory which would recognize that man was a part of nature, as subject to laws as any other part of nature, a theory which would explain human affects without invoking occult causes, a theory which would deal with the troublesome problem of the individual's relationship to the society of which he is a part, would explain why the individual must sometimes subordinate his prima facie interests as an individual to the interests of the whole, and explain what the limits on that subordination are, but also a theory which, while acknowledging the limits to control, would explain how men might control their affects.

12. THE *CONATUS*

The key to all this is a doctrine Spinoza shares with Hobbes, though he puts it to uses Hobbes does not seem to have thought of: "Each thing, as far as it can by its own power, strives to persevere in its being" (IIIP6). "Striving" is my preferred way of translating the word Spinoza uses, *conatus*, a word some render by "endeavor," which has the advantage of bringing out the Hobbesian associations of the term.[22] *Conatus* does normally suggest "trying," "making an effort," terms which in turn suggest that the thing trying has some conception of a goal it wants to achieve. But *conatus* also has a technical use in Cartesian physics—in the phrase *conatus ad motum*—to refer to the tendency bodies have to persist in a state either of rest or of uniform motion in a straight line. In that usage it does not imply any thought on the part of the thing "striving" (see *Principles* III, 56), and hence does not imply a goal the thing literally *wants* to achieve. This is just the way bodies will in fact act unless they are restrained by an external cause. Spinoza's usage is influenced by that Cartesian usage. As I read IIIP6, it states a principle which applies to *any* thing whatever.[23] Though Spinoza's panpsychism commits him to the view that each thing, no matter how simple, has a mind (in the sense that there is in God an idea of that thing), he surely doesn't think very simple things, like stones, have minds sufficiently like a human mind that they have any conception of where they are going when they are in motion. So they must lack anything like what we would call a desire to get there.[24]

What, exactly, does P6 say each thing will do? To the extent that it is not prevented from doing so by something external to it, it will do what would maintain it in existence in its present state, i.e., if doing X would maintain a thing in existence, then it will do X, if it is not interfered with.[25] This does not imply that the thing has a conception of X as maintaining it in existence. For very simple things, like a stone lying at rest on the ground, the thing's self-maintaining activity may consist in nothing more than the fact that its parts maintain that constant proportion of motion and rest which gives them their cohesion. For more complex things, things physically complex enough to have minds capable of self-consciousness, and of a conception of the future, the thing will be aware of its activity and of the result it is attaining by that activity.

13. DERIVING THE *CONATUS* DOCTRINE

Why does Spinoza think P6 is true? It's a striking fact about this proposition[26] that Spinoza does not seem to connect it very well with the propositions, axioms and definitions which have gone before it. He begins the demonstration by citing IP25C, paraphrased to read:

> Singular things are modes by which God's attributes are expressed in a certain and determinate way,

which is in turn glossed (via IP34) to read:

> Singular things are things that express, in a certain and determinate way, God's power, by which God is and acts.

It's not immediately obvious what the relevance of these propositions is, though I shall suggest later that they are not as idle as they seem. Then Spinoza cites IIIP4:

No thing can be destroyed except through an external cause;

and IIIP5 ("Things are of a contrary nature, i.e., cannot be in the same subject, insofar as one can destroy the other"), paraphrased to read:

Each thing is opposed to everything which can take its existence away.

These two steps apparently give us a short and simple argument: P5, which is supposed to directly follow from P4, is in turn supposed to directly entail P6.

Some find Spinoza's use of P5 suspicious.[27] I agree. But is it necessary to worry about this detail of the actual demonstration? Might we not take P6 as following directly from P4? Sometimes (e.g., in KV I, v, 1) that's what Spinoza himself seems to do. Why not? P4 says that if a thing is destroyed, it must be destroyed by an external cause. P6 says that each particular thing will do, to the extent that it is not prevented from doing so by something external to it, what would maintain it in existence in its present state. To imagine P6 false, we would have to imagine that, without any external interference, a thing does what will not maintain it in existence in its present state, i.e., something which would destroy it. And it does seem that this would violate P4.[28]

14. THE IMPOSSIBILITY OF SELF-DESTRUCTION

But P4 does not seem to be well-argued for, or, for that matter, true. Not well-argued for, because the 'demonstration' first proclaims that the proposition "is evident through itself" (*per se patet*), and then proceeds to offer an argument for it no step of which is a prior proposition, axiom or definition. Not true, because the proposition seems to be open to numerous counter-examples. Let us put aside counter-examples which might be controversial. In IVP20S Spinoza will argue that suicides are always "defeated by causes external and contrary to their nature." If his defense of that is persuasive,[29] then suicides will not constitute a genuine counter-example to P4. But there seem to be simpler and less controversial cases. Imagine a candle, burning on Spinoza's table as he works late at night on this part of the *Ethics*. Will it not, if left to itself, burn itself out, and thereby destroy itself? Some scholars have thought that Spinoza's answer to this would be "no." I think they are wrong, but I leave argument on that point to the notes.[30] Here I simply assert that the correct analysis of this proposed counter-example, from Spinoza's point of view, is that a burning candle is already a thing which has been acted on by an external cause—whatever lit the candle—and that its burning itself out must be seen as the effect of that cause.

Why does Spinoza think that any such example must be open to that kind of analysis? It may help here to look at the argument Spinoza offers for P4. It runs as follows:

> The definition of any thing affirms and does not deny the thing's essence, *or* it posits the thing's essence, and does not take it away. So while we attend only to the thing itself, and not to external causes, we will not be able to find anything in it which could destroy it.

Granted that none of the claims made here is, or could in any obvious way be, justified by citation of prior propositions, axioms or definitions, what does this argument tell us about Spinoza's reasons for holding P4?

Clearly the concepts of definition and essence are central to the argument. Earlier Spinoza had defined "essence" as "that which, being given, the thing itself is necessarily posited and which, being taken away, the thing itself is necessarily taken away" (IID2). This is helpful only to the extent that we are already clear about what constitutes "the thing itself," and it is not easy to see that Spinoza ever says anything useful about that notion. And he never defines "definition." But it may be helpful at this point to recall that Spinoza has a special theory about definitions, a theory he does not develop in the *Ethics* itself, but which he seems to be presupposing at this point.[31] What we might ordinarily regard as a satisfactory definition he will not count as satisfactory. His example is geometrical. Suppose the ordinary definition of a circle is that it is a closed curve all the points on which are equidistant from a given point. This does not tell us how a circle might be produced, and Spinoza thinks a satisfactory definition should do that, that it should embody a causal theory about how a circle might be constructed. So we might define a circle as a figure produced by the rotation of a line around a point. Spinoza thinks that if you define a circle in that way you will be able to see why circles have the properties they do, such as the property ordinarily used to define the circle. This may help to explain why, in the demonstration of P4, Spinoza speaks of the definition of a thing as affirming its essence. We must imagine the definition of a thing as a formula which describes a process by which a thing of that kind might be produced, as stating conditions which would lead to the existence of a thing of that kind, i.e., of a thing having all the properties common and peculiar to that kind of thing. So as long as we focus on that formula, we will, of course, find nothing which would entail the non-existence of the thing.

Of course, I have been imagining, as Spinoza typically does, that the definition will be the definition of a *kind* of thing. In order to apply that theory to P4 we have to assume that the definition is the definition of an individual thing, not of a kind, that it describes a process by which that very thing might be produced, a definition which will enable us to account for all the properties which that thing must have in order to be that thing. I don't imagine that Spinoza would in fact be able to tell us, in the case of any particular individual possessing an interesting degree of complexity, what those properties might be, or what the process which produced them would be. The theory of individuals developed in Part II after P13S seems to be a gesture in the direction of such an account, an attempt to give a general idea how it might go.[32] But it leaves unanswered a lot of questions about just what properties are essential to individuals.

15. THE ACTUAL ESSENCE OF THE THING

Still, one way of reading IIIP7 might be as a proposal to count as part of the essence of an individual any activity which can be understood to follow from its striving for self-preservation. P7 says:

> The striving by which each thing strives to persevere in its being is nothing but the actual essence of the thing.

'Activities' which cannot be understood to follow from the striving for self-preservation, as my scare-quotes are intended to suggest, are not properly activities. We are not, strictly speaking, active insofar as we behave in that way, but passive, acted on by things external to us (IIID2).[33] Note that in the demonstration of P7 Spinoza identifies the individual's striving for self-preservation with its power. Earlier (P6D) he had spoken mysteriously of singular things as expressions of God's power. I suggest that he thinks of the essence of an individual as a power or force, tending toward self-preservation, a force whose degree can be measured by the extent to which the individual actually does maintain itself (cf. IVPP2-5).

It might be objected at this point that to say this is to make the *conatus* doctrine trivially true.[34] If any failure of self-maintenance is going to be taken as an indication of passivity, of the action of something external on the individual, then of course it will be true that each thing, so far as it can, by its own power, strives to persevere in its being. But this, it may be said, is no more informative than telling us that all real Americans love the sting of battle and then dealing with apparent counter-examples by saying that the Americans in question are not real Americans.

I think this is too hasty an objection. The same thing might be said of the inertial principle in Newtonian mechanics, i.e., the principle which says that bodies will continue in their state of rest, or of uniform motion in a straight line, unless acted on by a net external force. Philosophers of science have frequently puzzled over its precise status, wondering whether it is intended as an analytic truth or an empirical generalization, open to refutation by counter-examples. I take it that the correct response in that case is to say that the principle cannot be judged in isolation from the other assumptions of Newtonian mechanics. If the inertial principle is part of a system of laws which gives precision to the otherwise open-ended idea of action by an external force, which specifies the ways in which forces might act, then it has content. I think there is no reason in principle why the same should not be said of Spinoza's *conatus* doctrine. The doctrine will have content to the extent that it can be integrated into a systematic psychology which yields testable results.

16. ANTECEDENTS OF THE *CONATUS* DOCTRINE

As we have seen, Spinoza is rather casual about proving the *conatus* doctrine. One reason for that may be that he found versions of the principle widely accepted by previous philosophers. We've already seen how Hobbes made an analogous principle the foundation of his political theory. But arguably Descartes too had recognized this principle. In the last chapter we saw that the basic bodily sensations of hunger, thirst, and pain were clear indications of the unity of mind and body, that they displayed a concern which the mind necessarily has for the needs and integrity of the body, a concern intelligible only on the hypothesis that mind and body are one. We might now regard these primitive desires for food, drink, and the avoidance of injury as expressions of the individual's basic striving for self-preservation. The facts which led Descartes to contend that the mind is not lodged in the body as a sailor in a ship are among the facts which make it plausible to ascribe a striving for self-preservation to the body. Again, to the extent that Descartes may be said to have a theory of good and evil, it seems that he identifies the good with the useful.[35] And as we have seen (§6), his account of what is useful to us does stress what helps to preserve the body and to make it more perfect. Insofar as he thinks that we have a natural tendency to pursue what we perceive to be good (AT VII, 166), the connections he makes between the good and the useful, and between the useful and self-preservation, imply a natural tendency to pursue our own preservation.

Similarly the Stoics made a version of the *conatus* doctrine a fundamental principle of human nature, arguing against the Epicurean insistence on the primacy of the desire for pleasure:

> As soon as a living thing is born it feels an attachment for itself and an inclination to preserve itself and its condition, and to love those things which tend to preserve its condition, while it is averse to its destruction and to those things which seem to lead to destruction. (Cicero, *De finibus* III, v)

Spinoza's version of this principle neatly reconciles Stoic and Epicurean, insofar as it incorporates into the *conatus* a striv-

ing not only for self-preservation, but also for greater perfection, understood as an increase in power of action, which is
what Spinoza understands joy to be (IIIP11 and P11S). The
idea seems to be that a striving for self-preservation must,
given that powerful external forces are ranged against us
(E IVA1), also be a striving for increased power of action.[36]
Insofar as we can plausibly take an increase of power of action
to be felt as pleasurable, we can understand the Epicureans to
have seen part of the truth about human nature. Spinoza
might well say of the Epicureans, what he says in another context of the Hebrews (E IIP7S), that they had seen the truth of
his philosophy as if through a cloud.

17. THE *CONATUS* DOCTRINE AS A FOUNDATION FOR PSYCHOLOGY

Spinoza had complained about Descartes that he tried to explain the affects through their first causes, but offered, in the
end, a hypothesis more occult than any occult quality. You
can see the grounds for this complaint if you reflect on the
definition of love Descartes offers in the *Passions of the Soul*
(§79). It is an emotion of the soul caused by the movement of
the animal spirits which, via the pineal gland, move the soul
to join itself voluntarily to objects which appear agreeable to
it. The cause is identified only in terms of the kind of effect it
has, and this is no more informative than telling us that opium
puts people to sleep because it has a dormitive virtue, where
nothing more can be said about the dormitive virtue except
that it is a power to put people to sleep. Had Spinoza chosen
to single out Hobbes for criticism in the Preface to Part III, he
might have complained that Hobbes does not even attempt to
explain love through its first cause, since he defines it simply
as that species of desire which commonly involves a present
object (*Lev* vi, 3).

Spinoza's account of love is meant to be genuinely explanatory, according to the model of explanation he accepted, which requires deduction of general laws from even more fundamental principles. In the case of love, the explanation goes like this: if each thing, so far as it can, strives to persevere in its being, then the mind will do this as well (P9); because of the parallelism between mind and body, the idea of anything which increases the body's power of acting increases the mind's power of thinking (P11); such changes in the perfection of the mind (in its power of thinking) are felt as joy (P11S);[37] hence, so far as it can, the mind will strive to imagine things which increase the body's power of acting (P12); so, if we understand love to be joy, accompanied by the idea of an external cause, i.e., a passage to a greater perfection, accompanied by the idea of something external as the cause of that passage, we will understand why a lover necessarily strives to have the thing he loves, the thing which causes him joy, present (P13S). Accepting Spinoza's definition of love (along with his definition of joy) enables us to deduce generalizations about lovers (the properties of love) from the fundamental principles of nature, i.e., from the *conatus* doctrine. This illustrates a pattern which is followed throughout Part III of the *Ethics*. There is a constant interplay between definitions and generalizations about human behavior, with the definitions being justified by their role in linking the generalizations with the more fundamental assumptions.

We can't here follow Spinoza through the detail of his deductions of psychological generalizations from his initial assumptions. But there are two particular claims we should note because of their systematic importance. One of the key features of human behavior, according to Spinoza, is the fact that we are apt to suffer what he calls vacillation of mind, and what we would nowadays call ambivalence. Spinoza's main explanation of this relies on the principle of association of

ideas. Things we have experienced together we tend to asso-
ciate with one another afterward (IIP18). So if a thing has a
quality we have associated with a certain affect, even though
it is not itself the cause of that affect, we will tend to feel the
affect anyway (IIIPP14-16). We may do this even in cases
where the thing in other respects tends to cause us an opposite
affect (P17). So we are apt to experience conflicting emotions
with regard to the thing. But Spinoza notes that this is only
one route to his conclusion, the easiest way he had of deducing
this particular affect. He does not deny that vacillations of
mind for the most part arise from an object which is itself the
cause of both the contrary affects:

> For the human body . . . is composed of a great many in-
> dividuals of different natures, and so . . . it can be affected
> in a great many different ways by one and the same body.
> And on the other hand, because one and the same body
> can be affected in many ways [in the sense that it can have
> many different qualities], it will also be able to affect one
> and the same part of the body in many different ways.
> From this we easily conceive that one and the same object
> can be the cause of many contrary affects. (P17S)

This ambivalence was an extremely important feature of human psychology for Spinoza, prompting a rare but powerful
metaphor at the end of Part III:

> From what has been said it is clear that we are driven
> about in many ways by external causes, and that, like
> waves on the sea, driven by contrary winds, we toss
> about, not knowing our outcome and fate. (P59S)

Spinoza's realism about the human emotions, his recognition
of the importance of conflict, was aided not only by his determinism, his insistence that the human mind is not a kingdom
within a kingdom, insulated by free will from the rest of na-

ture, but also by his materialism, his picture of the mind as the idea of the body, necessarily sharing in the complexity of its object. As we have seen, Descartes, conceiving of the mind as a simple substance, was unable to admit genuine ambivalence.

The other important feature of Spinozistic psychology we must note is his doctrine of the imitation of the affects, first stated in IIIP27: "If we imagine a thing like us, toward which we have had no affect, to be affected with some affect, we are thereby affected with a like affect." This is an attempt to explain such phenomena as pity (P27S), or feeling sadness because of the sadness of someone like us, and benevolence, defined as the desire to do good to someone we pity (P27C3S). I say "an attempt," because I agree with those critics who think the argument offered is not very successful.[38] It's striking that Spinoza's "demonstration" relies entirely on doctrines from Part II, as if this principle were independent of the *conatus* doctrine. We may naturally wonder whether Spinoza might have been able to mount a more plausible argument had he tried to construct it from materials in Part III.[39] But I won't attempt to decide that here. My main concern is with the important role this principle plays in Spinoza's system.

Part of the interest of the principle is that it provides—or helps to provide—a basis for human sociability which is less calculating than we find in Hobbes.[40] Spinoza does, of course, allow other ways in which pity can arise. It is natural for us to pity when those we love are affected with sadness (P21, 22S), and to feel a corresponding positive emotion when they are affected with joy (P22S). But P27 is designed to explain how we can feel compassion for others, feel their joys and sorrows, even when we have not had any prior affect for them, simply because they are like us. Of course, Spinoza does not explain how much similarity there must be before we feel this fellow-feeling, but I think it would be expecting too much of him to do that. It seems clear that this is a matter where individual differences are tremendous. Some will feel compassion on the basis of very little similarity, others will be able to identify only with a very limited circle of people very like themselves, and most will feel varying degrees of compassion depending on the degree of similarity.[41] Once we feel this compassion, of course, we acquire a personal interest in relieving the suffering of others. It will be to our advantage to act from benevolence (P27C3D). But the pity itself is prior to any calculations of self-interest.

It is characteristic of Spinoza's psychology, however, that he sees the imitation of the affects as a two-edged sword. The same property of human nature which gives rise to pity gives rise also to emulation (P27S), defined as feeling desire for a thing because someone like us desires the same thing. This can generate as much discord as benevolence generates harmony. It leads to ambition, the striving to act so as to please others (P29S) and to envy, in the case where the other person enjoys something only one can possess (P32S). But even an affect like ambition, when it does not lead us to do things injurious to ourselves or others, can promote harmony. The desire for approval can be a very positive force. One way of looking at Spinoza's psychology is that it attempts to deduce, from fundamental principles of human nature, both the tendencies to discord which make the state necessary, and the tendencies to harmony which make it possible.[42]

18. THE *CONATUS* AS A FOUNDATION FOR ETHICS

When the concepts of good and evil make their first appearance in the *Ethics*, in the Appendix to Part I (II / 81-83), and in Part III, the tenor of Spinoza's discussion of them is highly subjectivistic, much in the manner of Hobbes. So for example, he writes in IIIP9S that we neither strive for, nor will, neither want nor desire, anything because we judge it to be good; on the contrary, we judge something to be good because we strive for it, will it, want it, and desire it.

This echoes the *Leviathan* (vi, 7) and opposes the Cartesian doctrine that desire is a passion born of the consideration of good and evil (PA §57). Spinoza recognizes, as Hobbes did and Descartes did not, that the status of value judgments is problematic, that these judgments vary enormously from one individual to another, and that the variations are related to differences in the desires of the people concerned. As a good materialist, he believes that the differences in desire are a function of differences in corporeal constitution (IIIP56D, 59S). It is in this spirit that he writes in IIIP39S:

By good I here understand every kind of Joy, and whatever leads to it, and especially what satisfies any kind of longing, whatever that may be. And by evil [I understand here] every kind of sadness, and especially what frustrates longing.

When we say that something is good or evil, we are not ascribing any objective property to it, we are only signifying something about our own relation to it, roughly that we desire it or find it frustrating to our desires.

And yet much of the *Ethics* is concerned with making what appear to be value judgments. Spinoza tells us that the knowledge of God is the mind's greatest good (IVP28), that joy is not directly evil, but good, whereas sadness is directly evil (P41), that joy, love and desire can be excessive (PP43,44), that hate can never be good (P45), that hope and fear can never be good in themselves, though they may be good as a way of restraining excesses of joy and desire (P47), and so on. If these claims don't represent objective statements about the things with which they deal, are they not out of place in the *Ethics*, which is supposed to be demonstrative science on a par with geometry? If they are not objectively valid, why does Spinoza seem to regard them as dictates or commands of reason?

To understand the shift from the subjectivism of the early parts of the *Ethics* to the objectivism of the later parts, we need to begin by attending to the analysis of good and evil in the Preface to Part IV. There Spinoza offers an account of the concept of perfection, which starts, as he once said all conceptual analysis should (CM I, vi, 1 / 246 / 18ff), with the meaning the term "perfect" has in ordinary language. Etymologically, "perfect" means something which is done thoroughly or is finished. So if a person sees a house which is half built, he would correctly describe it as imperfect, whereas if it is finished, that would be a sufficient reason for calling it perfect. (This sounds much more natural in Latin than in English.) Ordinary usage is only the first word, however, not the last. Spinoza imagines that we developed a new usage from the old when we began to form general ideas, which we then took as models of judgment. Though we might not know, in the absence of information about the plans of its maker, whether a particular thing was really finished or not, we might nevertheless judge it to be perfect or imperfect, depending on whether or not it conformed well to our general idea of that kind of thing.

This will obviously make much more sense when we are dealing with things which actually do have a maker in an identifiable agent whose plans we might inquire about if we didn't already know them. Our general idea of the kind of thing in question is at least some kind of guide to the actual intentions of the maker. But Spinoza thinks we have illegitimately extended to natural things, like men, a practice sensible only in connection with artificial things, like houses. At any rate, the practice is not sensible in connection with natural things once we have given up the idea that all things in nature have been crafted by a purposive agent (as the argument of the Appendix to Part I has urged us to do). So our ordinary use of the concept of perfection in connection with natural things is apparently undermined by its presupposition of divine teleology. And if this were not bad enough, our ordinary moral judgments have the further defect that the general ideas we use as standards of judgment vary from one individual to another, as the individual's experience of members of the kind varies (cf. IIP40S1). What holds for "perfect" and "imperfect" holds equally for "good" and "bad," which likewise imply reference to a standard, though only a greater or lesser approximation to the standard, not complete agreement with it.

Now this seems to me a remarkably suggestive analysis of the meaning of the evaluative terms in question—much more promising than the Hobbesian analyses of the earlier parts of the *Ethics*. I think it compares favorably with much which has been written in our own century.[43] But so far it seems only to raise all over again the issue of the subjectivity of moral judgments. If those judgments presuppose reference to a general idea which is to serve as a standard of judgment, and if the general ideas different people have of such things as men vary greatly from one person to another, with none of them having a privileged position as supplying the appropriate standard of judgment, how can our judgments—or rather how can the judgments Spinoza makes in the *Ethics*—pretend to any objective validity?

The answer, I think, lies in a passage toward the end of the Preface to Part IV, where Spinoza writes that although good and evil indicate nothing positive in things, considered in themselves, and are nothing more than notions we form because we compare things to one another,

> still, we must retain these words. For . . . we desire to form an idea of man, as a model of human nature which

we may look to . . . In what follows, therefore, I shall understand by good what we know certainly is a means by which we may approach nearer and nearer to the model of human nature we set before ourselves, and by evil, what we certainly know prevents us from becoming like that model . . . (II / 208 / 15ff)

Spinoza says nothing further about this concept of a model of human nature which we may look to—at any rate the parts of the *Ethics* which follow contain nothing explicit about it. Nevertheless, I think we miss something if we dismiss it as unimportant.[44]

I take it that Spinoza's view is that we can form a general idea of a certain kind of person, and that once we have done so, that general idea sorts itself out from the other general ideas of man we might have as being the idea of a kind of person we necessarily desire to be. The most general characterization of that kind of person might be that he/she possesses much greater power of action than any other being a human is capable of becoming (cf. TdIE §§12-13). But we might equally well characterize that kind of person as free (cf. E IVPP67-73) or guided by reason. Though there is no explicit talk of models, the whole of Part IV of the *Ethics* is the construction of the idea of a model human being. And when we are told that cheerfulness is always good and melancholy always evil (P42), or that hate can never be good (P45), or that he who lives according to the guidance of reason strives, as far as he can, to repay the other's hate, anger and disdain toward him with love or nobility (P46), we are being told what kind of person to be, what things will be useful to us in becoming the kind of person we would necessarily desire to be if only we could form a clear conception of that kind of person. It is in this sense that the foundation of virtue is the striving to preserve one's being (P18S, II / 222 / 27). The feelings and behavior the *Ethics* recommends as good are necessary means to a necessary end. The whole project is highly Hobbesian, although I think it fair to say that Spinoza goes much further than Hobbes does in trying to show the utility of that portion of traditional morality which he retains.

19. THE UTILITY OF MAN

The general project of trying to show that a prudent concern for my own interests will lead me to behave justly, honorably, and generously to my fellow men is a Hobbesian one.[45] Hobbes would certainly have agreed with Spinoza that (potentially at least) nothing is more useful to man than man (P18S). But there is something quite distinctive about the way Spinoza supports this claim. It's not just that Spinoza takes the attempt to provide a deductive system far more seriously than Hobbes ever did, though that is true enough. There is a special Spinozistic flavor to the way in which this conclusion is reached.

First of all, Spinoza does not appear, as Hobbes does, to see civil society as required by what man's rationality would lead him to in the state of nature. "If men lived according to the guidance of reason," Spinoza writes (IVP37S2), everyone would possess his natural rights "without injury to anyone else." Civil society is necessary as an arbiter between men because men are liable to affects which are capable of overpowering reason.

In large part this difference stems from a difference of opinion about what is truly good, or what would be desired by a rational man, a man who was thinking clearly about his own interests. Hobbes sees men as necessarily competing for such things as honor, riches and power (in the sense of dominion over others—cf. *Lev* xi, 2-3), goods which cannot be shared without at least one of those who shares having less than he would have had otherwise. He does not think there is any such thing as the *summum bonum*, or greatest good, "spoken of in the books of the old moral philosophers" (*Lev* xi, 1). There is no such thing as attaining peace of mind. "Felicity is a continual progress of the desire, from one object to the other, the attaining of the former being but the way to the later" (ibid., cf. EL I, vii, 7).

Spinoza, on the other hand, believes there is a *summum bonum*, the knowledge and love of God (IVP28, VP20D), which leads to true peace of mind (VP42S) and which is such that it can in principle be shared by many without anyone's portion thereby being diminished (IVP36). In fact, I think Spinoza would say that the special importance he attaches to friendship stems from the fact that as friends share their knowledge with one another, each finds that his own knowledge is increased (IVApp9,12). To prevent misunderstanding, I should stress that when Spinoza speaks of the knowledge of God as the *summum bonum*, I take him to be understanding that phrase very broadly, not as limited to the kind of knowledge which would more conventionally be thought of as knowledge of God. Any kind of scientific understanding of any subject matter will count as knowledge of God (VPP24,30). So for example, Freudian psychology, if it genuinely provided a scientific understanding of man, would be knowledge of God.

One of the most eloquent passages in the *Ethics* is, in effect, a hymn to the joys of civilization:

> It is the part of a wise man . . . to refresh and restore himself in moderation with pleasant food and drink, with scents, with the beauty of green plants, with decoration, music, sports, the theater and other things of this kind, which anyone can use without injury to another. For the human body is composed of a great many parts of different natures, which constantly require new and varied

nourishment, so that the whole body may be equally capable of all the things which can follow from its nature, and hence, so that the mind also may be equally capable of understanding many things. (IVP45S)

Spinoza is no ascetic. Believing as he does in the dependence of the mind on the body, he recognizes the importance of satisfying the genuine needs of the body as a way of attaining the greatest good. And he recognizes that many of these goods would be unattainable if individual men had to rely on their own powers, if men did not help one another (IVApp28). Whereas the emphasis in Hobbes is on security against the threat of violent death, and the "delights of society" are painted in cynical terms—"all society is either for gain or for glory" (DC i, 2)—Spinoza offers a much more attractive (and realistic) picture of human society.

20. SPINOZA AS A PRECURSOR OF NIETZSCHE

Earlier I said that Spinoza goes much further than Hobbes does in trying to show the utility of that portion of traditional morality which he retains. But Spinoza goes beyond Hobbes also in openly rejecting certain elements of traditional Christian morality, in proposing what Nietzsche was later to call a revaluation of values. By and large Hobbes is content to show that a prudent regard for our own interest would lead us to practice a wide range of traditional social virtues: to keep promises we have made, to be grateful to those who have done us a service, to strive to accommodate ourselves to our fellows, and so on. If he rejects any of the traditional virtues (as the tone of his social analysis might lead us to suspect), he is discreet enough not to say so explicitly.

Much of Spinoza's moral teaching is in that Hobbesian spirit of accommodation, as when he argues that he who lives according to the guidance of reason strives, as far as he can, to repay the other's hate, anger, and disdain toward him, with love, or nobility. (IVP46)

But much of it, particularly in the later propositions of Part IV, is not. So, for example, he writes in P50 that "in a man who lives according to the guidance of reason, pity is evil of itself, and useless." The first part of this is not surprising, given Spinoza's initial assumptions. IIIP22S had defined pity as a sadness which has arisen from an injury which has occurred to someone else. But to classify pity as a species of sadness, as a transition to a lesser perfection, to less power of action, is to condemn it as something which in itself is evil (IVP41), something whose evil is not redeemed by its concern for the welfare of another.[46] The second part is, initially, surprising. For you might think that Spinoza would recognize some utility in pity, insofar as it leads us to strive to free the object of our pity from his suffering (IIIP27C3), and thereby to encourage his gratitude and friendship towards us. But in the man who is guided by reason, this motivation is unnecessary. For if he is truly guided by reason, he will want the good he seeks for himself for others also (IVP37). Only to the extent that men are subject to the affects, is it useful, and hence, good, for them to be moved by pity.

In a similar vein, Spinoza opposes humility not to pride, but to self-esteem, which he pronounces to be the highest thing we can hope for (IVP52S). Self-esteem is a joy, humility a sadness, each arising from the fact that a man considers himself and his power of acting (IIIDefAff25,26), the former from considering what he can do, the latter from considering what he cannot do, the limitations on his power of acting. Humility is no virtue (IVP53),[47] and neither is repentance (IVP54). The latter is doubly irrational, both insofar as it is sadness, and insofar as it is that particular species of sadness which arises from our

127

belief that we have done something bad from a free decision of our will (IIIDefAff27). Like pity, these affects may have some utility for the many, who are not guided by the dictate of reason (IVP54S), but they are among the things the free man will strive to be free of.[48]

Again, in spite of the doctrine of the eternity of the mind, Spinoza sets himself resolutely against that view of the world which sees this life as a preparation for the life to come: "Blessedness is not the reward of virtue, but virtue itself; nor do we enjoy it because we restrain our lusts; on the contrary, because we enjoy it, we are able to restrain them" (VP42). Blessedness is something we enjoy in this life, if we live our lives according to the dictates of reason, not something we hope to attain in a life to come by acting contrary to our nature in this life.[49]

21. THE MASTERY OF THE PASSIONS

In the summer of 1881 Nietzsche wrote an excited postcard to Overbeck to express his amazement at having discovered a precursor in Spinoza:

> Not only is his over-all tendency like mine—making knowledge the *most powerful* affect—but in five main points of his doctrine I recognize myself; this most unusual and loneliest thinker is closest to me in precisely these matters: he denies the freedom of the will, teleology, the moral world order, the unegoistic, and evil . . .[50]

Nietzsche certainly recognized the affinities we have been exploring in the preceding section. But in this final section I want to focus on that over-all tendency Nietzsche alludes to here: making knowledge the most powerful affect. From Spinoza's point of view, this may be inexact, since I don't think Spinoza would count knowledge as an affect at all, but it certainly is true that Spinoza ascribes to knowledge great power over the things he would count as affects. "We shall determine, by the mind's knowledge alone, the remedies for the affects," he writes in the Preface to Part v (II / 283 / 23).

Spinoza describes the way this is supposed to work in the early propositions of Part v (from P1 to P20, with a helpful summary in P20S). There he presents a variety of remedies for the affects, of which I shall focus on only two, as being particularly important and suggestive. But before discussing particular cases, I think we need to note that none of these remedies, either individually or taken in conjunction with the others, is meant to be a cure-all. One of the things Spinoza is most anxious to insist on, one of the things he sees as setting him apart from previous authors who have tried to find remedies for the affects, most notably from Descartes and the Stoics (vPref, II / 277 / 17-278 / 4), is that we do not, and in the nature of things cannot, have absolute power over the affects. Human power over the affects is limited (IVA1). In any given case, there may be nothing we can do to control a harmful affect. And even in a favorable case, the best we can do may be nothing more than to moderate or restrain the affect.[51]

The first of the two remedies I want to discuss is that offered in vP2:

If we separate emotions or affects from the thought of an external cause, and join them to other thoughts, then the love or hate toward the external cause is destroyed, as are the vacillations of mind arising from these affects.

Here Spinoza capitalizes on one of the strong points of his psychology. Unlike such predecessors as Descartes and such successors as Hume, he defines most of his affects in such a way as to make clear that they involve an element of belief, and that different affects may be distinguished from one another by the different beliefs they involve.[52] So when Spinoza defines hate as sadness, accompanied by the idea of an external cause, we are to understand that in hate the object of our hate is thought of as the cause of our sadness.[53] Indignation is also a form of sadness, and indeed, a form of hate, but in the particular case of indignation the cause of our sadness is thought of as causing sadness to us by causing harm to someone or something else.

This way of thinking about the affects has a number of advantages. It explains why it makes sense to talk about the affects as being rationally justified or not (since the beliefs they involve may or may not be rationally justified). And it explains what the connection is between the affect and its object (viz. that the object of the affect is the object the component belief is about). But the most important advantage for our purposes is that it opens the way for a form of cognitive therapy. If a certain belief is an essential component in a particular affect, and if we can destroy that belief, or weaken it, then we will have destroyed or weakened the affect of which it is a component.

Of course this technique will provide a remedy for the affects only to the extent to which we have some control over our beliefs. Certainly Spinoza does not think we can believe or disbelieve at will (IIP49S).[54] Ridding ourselves of a belief may involve a difficult process of looking again at our evidence for the belief, testing alternative theories which might explain that evidence equally well, criticizing the logic by which we have arrived at the belief, and so on. A person I had thought friendly to me did not return my greeting this morning. Perhaps I was wrong to think he bore me good will. Perhaps something has happened to change his mind about me. Or perhaps he was just preoccupied with other matters. Often the beliefs that matter most to our happiness involve treacherous inferences from other people's behavior to their mental states. If, as I would be inclined to think, many harmful emotions are

based on false or questionable beliefs,[55] then attacking the beliefs which provide their basis seems a promising strategy. The
person who has the belief may not be able, without help from
others, to see that his belief is false or questionable. But I take
it that one of the services a good therapist can provide is to
give you a different perspective on things which, without his
aid, you would believe uncritically.

It might be objected[56] that even if we do have this kind of
indirect control over our beliefs, it will not in general help to
eliminate the belief from the affect. The thought of an external
cause is at best only one element in an affect, and it is not
necessarily present in such basic affects as joy and sadness.
Suppose I hate someone, in the sense that I feel sadness and I
believe the other person to be the cause of my sadness. Suppose further that I am wrong about the cause of my sadness,
and that I come to see that belief as false, without acquiring
any new belief about the cause of my sadness. What I feel no
longer counts as hate, but I am still sad. What have I gained?
It seems that cognitive therapy will be useful only to the extent
that it is my belief about something external which is the immediate cause of the non-cognitive element in my affect, i.e.,
of the sadness. In such cases—e.g., when my false belief that
someone is ill-disposed towards me is the cause of my sadness—removing my belief may also remove the sadness which
it causes. But it won't generally be the case that my belief
about something external is the immediate cause of my sadness. Sometimes things external to me cause me to be sad
without affecting my beliefs, and in those cases it seems that
the most I can hope for is to replace one harmful affect (hate)
with another (sadness).

Still, if we have realistic expectations about what the remedies for the affects can do, we should not consider it a serious
weakness in P2 that it works only in some cases. And even in
the cases where we merely replace one harmful affect with an-

other, that may represent significant progress. For if the argument of Part III is correct, hate is a more harmful affect than simple sadness. If I hate someone, that affect inclines me to try to harm him in (what I believe to be) retaliation (IIIP39). To the extent that I succeed, and he perceives me as harming him, he will hate me and be inclined to harm me in return. Hate sets up a vicious cycle of harm and retaliation. Mere sadness has no such side effects.

In this first remedy for the affects, knowledge works by showing us the inadequacy of particular ideas which are integral to certain of the affects. In the second remedy for the affects which I propose to discuss, knowledge is supposed to work by revealing to us the necessity of all things:

> VP6: Insofar as the mind understands all things as necessary, it has a greater power over the affects, or is less acted on by them.

Since Spinoza thinks that it is the nature of reason to understand things as necessary, and not as contingent (IIP44), it follows that the more we have rational understanding of things, the less we suffer from affects in regard to them. Spinoza emphasizes in the scholium to P6 that our knowledge of the necessity of things will be a more effective remedy if it is not merely knowledge of the general truth that all things are necessary, but knowledge of the necessity of the particular thing in question, knowledge generated, presumably, by knowledge of the causal process by which it was brought about.

I find this to be a plausible position, whatever doubts we may entertain about the way Spinoza demonstrates it. In IIIP48 Spinoza argues that if we experience an affect of hate towards someone, that affect will be lessened if we find that that person was not the sole cause of our sadness. The thought seems to be that if we discovered that our sadness was caused, not by the object of our hate at all, but by some other object, we would automatically hate the other object, and cease to hate the original object of our hate. That much seems to be a fairly straightforward consequence of the definition of hate. But Spinoza thinks it must follow that if we should discover that the responsibility for our sadness was divided between two causes, the hate would be divided proportionally. Arguably[57] this tacitly assumes that I have a fixed quantity of hate to distribute among its objects, so that the more objects of hate there are, the less I hate each one. But it's not clear to me that that assumption is wrong. If the total quantity of my hate were increased by additional information about the cause of my sadness, then my sadness would have to be increased simply by increasing my information about the causation of my sadness, and there doesn't seem to be any reason why that should be true.

The more serious objection seems to be that if we redistribute our affects over a wider range of objects, we do not necessarily reduce our total level of affect, and that vP6 seems to promise that as a consequence of our coming to see things as necessary.[58] But perhaps this is again a case of our having unrealistic expectations of the remedies for the affects. Spinoza wants the mind to have greater power over the affects, but it does not follow that he wants the mind to be free of affects, anymore than Descartes did. Joy, after all, is something we necessarily strive for, something good in itself, not something Spinoza would want to diminish unless it happened to have bad overall consequences (IVPP41-44). And the same would hold for affects essentially involving joy (and not essentially involving sadness), such as love. So perhaps we should see the goal of vP6 to be an alteration of the balance between positive and negative affects, in favor of the positive affects, rather than a decrease in the total level of affect. If that is the goal, then a redistribution of negative affects, like hate, over a wider range of objects might be helpful in the long run, even if it did

not immediately reduce the total level of negative affect. Suppose I hate X, but come to see his harmful behavior towards
me as caused by Y. I now hate Y also, though by hypothesis
the total quantity of my hate has not increased. I hate X less
than I did before, and Y more than I did before. This may
make it harder for me to deal with Y in a constructive way,
but it will make it easier for me to deal with X. When I hated
him more strongly, I was more inclined to do things which
would harm him, and to perpetuate the vicious cycle of harm
and retaliation. Suppose, as might often happen, particularly
among people who have close relations with each other, that
my feelings towards X and his feelings towards me are a mix
of love and hate. If my hate towards him is diminished, that
will make it easier for me to act on my positive feelings towards him, and to respond appropriately to his positive actions towards me. We may be able to turn a cycle of harm and
retaliation into a cycle of benefit and reciprocation. "Hate is
increased by being returned, but can be destroyed by love"
(IIIP43). In favorable circumstances, the end result could be
that my initial hate for X is not merely diminished, but elimi-
nated altogether, with a consequent reduction in my total level
of negative affect, and a more favorable balance of positive
and negative affect.

Someone might object that these benefits are purchased at
the cost of increasing my negative feelings towards Y, and that
there may be similar, but in that case harmful, side effects of
that change. And so there may be. But it is also possible that
there will not be. If Y is someone with whom I do not have to
deal (a dead parent, perhaps, or a schoolteacher in a town far
away), the fact that I have come to hate that person may have
no further consequences. Circumstances must be favorable for
this remedy to work in the way that I have suggested. But
sometimes circumstances are favorable. So sometimes Spinoz-

istic therapy will work. And that, I think, is the most that we can hope of any therapy.

My account of Spinozistic therapy has stressed the limitations, both of what it hopes to achieve and of the circumstances in which it can be expected to work. This seems to me more true to the spirit of Spinoza's philosophy than those passages in the *Ethics* which may suggest that our victory over the passions may be easy. "All things excellent are as difficult as they are rare" (VP42S). But to say that our power is limited is not to deny that it is worthwhile to strive mightily to exercise such power as we have. The harmful affects can be very harmful indeed, and we must do what we can if we are to truly pursue our own interest.

NOTES

❦

1. See Wolfson, p. 3. (For publication details of works cited in shortened form, see the Bibliographical Note, pp. viiiff.)

2. Bennett writes: "I am encouraged in [my inattention to Spinoza's philosophical ancestry] by the massive work in which Wolfson places Spinoza in a densely described medieval setting: the labour and learning are awesome, but the *philosophical* profit is almost nil" (Bennett, p. 16). I agree that Wolfson's execution of his program is profoundly disappointing. But I do not take that fact to impugn the project of trying to see Spinoza as responding to his predecessors. Bennett himself does attend to Spinoza's ancestry ("I shall make much of Descartes as a bequeather of problems which Spinoza tried to solve"—p. 15). But I don't think he, or any other writer on Spinoza has exploited the possibilities of this approach as fully as would be useful. And I think Bennett is sometimes led astray by his neglect of the medieval background. E.g., his treatment of teleology (in §§50-51) seems to me to suffer from a failure to recognize that in Spinoza's time the battle against medieval views had not yet been won. I discuss this in more detail in a forthcoming article, "On Bennett's Spinoza: the Issue of Teleology."

3. The usual assumption has been that the *Short Treatise* is the earliest of Spinoza's works and was written in the late 1650s. But recently this has become a matter for dispute, largely because of the work of Mignini. For details see my edition of Spinoza's works (publication details below). I am inclined to accept Mignini's view that the *Treatise on the Emendation of the Intellect* preceded the *Short Treatise*.

4. Bennett writes: "I shall not attend much to the *Short Treatise* ... its status is dubious, its content confused, its fit with the rest of [Spinoza's] work uncomfortable. These factors and its probable early date make this work a feeble aid to understanding Spinoza's mature thought" (Bennett, p. 7). Though I agree that the *Short Treatise* is a very difficult work, I still think it a mistake to dismiss it in that way.

137

For example, it seems to me that a comparison of the *Ethics* with the *Short Treatise* is very helpful in coming to an understanding of Spinoza's thought about the divine attributes, or about the infinite modes, or about the relation between mind and body, to mention only a few examples.

5. Bennett, p. 41. Bennett offers this account of dualism only as a crude first approximation and devotes the next few pages of his *Study* to refining it, arriving at a precise statement on p. 45. The dualism he finally attributes to Spinoza is a dualism of concepts rather than properties: roughly again, that, apart from a sharply defined class of transcategorical concepts (which includes logical, numerical and temporal concepts), all our concepts fall into two categories, such that every member of each category is logically connected with every other member of that category and is not logically connected with any member of the other category. Two concepts are "logically connected" with each other if they are the termini of some sequence of concepts each of which either entails or is entailed by its immediate neighbors.

6. Bennett (§§31-32) suggests that Spinoza's real reason for accepting the doctrine of parallelism lies not in the demonstrations of IIP7 or IIP3, but in the fact that parallelism is required by the denial of interaction, to which Spinoza is committed by his dualism. In a forthcoming article, "Le corps et l'esprit: Du *Court traité* à l'*Ethique*," I argue that this cannot be right, since the Spinoza of the *Short Treatise* accepts parallelism, while admitting interaction between mind and body.

7. Bennett, pp. 41, 70. Bennett points out that Spinoza's monism about substance does not contrast with a dualism held by Descartes, since Descartes thinks there are not two, but indefinitely many substances. But he allows that the mind-body identity thesis might be used to define a monism which would contrast with a dualism held by Descartes. Descartes will view a human being as two things, each of which has properties radically different in kind from the other. Spinoza will view a human being as one thing, which possesses properties of two radically different kinds. In comments on the ms. of this book he writes that Spinoza "thought that a single thing can be both extended and thinking, and indeed that the only items that think are also extended. He could easily express his position by saying 'There are only extended things,' and that is indeed (in a way) a precursor

of materialism (of a kind). That much is all agreeable to me, and endorsed in my book."

8. See Donagan, p. 90. Donagan offers, as an example of one of Descartes' Copernican affirmations, his doctrine "that the Earth, if seen from the heaven, would only seem like a planet, smaller than Jupiter or Saturn" (III, 8). An even better example might have been the doctrine that the Sun, too, does not move from one place in the heavens to another (III, 21). I should note for the record that the *first* draft of these lectures was written in the fall of 1983 as a paper for a meeting of the Illinois Philosophical Association honoring Alan Donagan. That paper, which criticized his contribution to the Kennington volume, sketched many of the ideas developed in chapters 1 and 2. So originally I had Donagan more in mind than Bennett.

9. Before we can decide what to think about it, we need to decide how sincere Descartes is in affirming that the Earth does not move. Here it is relevant to consider that some eleven years before Descartes published the *Principles* he had been on the point of publishing an explicitly Copernican treatise (*Le monde*) which he withheld when he learned of the condemnation of Galileo. This makes it natural for Donagan to talk about a "formal disavowal" of Copernicanism and suggests that Descartes uses III, 28, merely as a device for avoiding trouble with the Inquisition. But whatever external pressures might have been working on Spinoza would not have inclined him to make a dualistic philosophy sound monistic. Spinoza's monism was one of the things most apt to get him in trouble with the authorities, since it threatened the orthodox doctrine of the immortality of the soul.

10. I allude here to an essay by Stuart Hampshire, first published in the *Proceedings of the American Philosophical Association* for 1969 and subsequently reprinted in *Freedom of Mind and Other Essays*, Princeton: Princeton UP, 1971. Though my style of argument is very different, I find Hampshire's reading of Spinoza on this point very congenial, more so than anything which has appeared more recently.

11. See Curley (1), Bibliographical Note.

12. I've always felt uncomfortable with the interpretation offered in chapter 4 of Curley (1) and have not been surprised to see it come under attack (e.g., by Margaret Wilson, in her contribution to the Kennington anthology). While I think the account of Part I offered in the first chapter of this book is generally compatible with the account offered in the first three chapters of the earlier book, I am not sure

the account of Part II offered in the second chapter of this book is compatible with the account offered in the final chapter of the earlier book.

1. So, for instance, readers of Moore (ch. 1) should be struck by how much his Common Sense view of the world is a Cartesian view of the world.

2. My reference to the earliest *substantial* written works we have from Spinoza is meant to exclude the first dialogue of the KV but to include the rest of the text. I do not mean to disagree with Lachièze-Rey, whose work, though limited in its scope, still seems to be the most thorough examination of the development of Spinoza's thought, insofar as this can be inferred from a study of the *Short Treatise*. In my edition of Spinoza's works (I, 49n, 73n) I aligned myself with Freudenthal's view that both dialogues in the KV were later than the main body of the text. I now think Lachièze-Rey is right that the first dialogue is earlier than the main text, that it advances (in §9) a theory of the relation of the attributes to substance which is incompatible with the theory of the main body of the work (e.g., in I, vii, 10), that the influence of Descartes is reduced to a minimum in this dialogue, and that the dialogue shows the influence of a fundamental conviction of the unity of nature which Spinoza did not owe to Descartes, and which transformed the materials he did take from Descartes. All of this seems to me true and important. But it is equally true and important that as Spinoza's system began to take shape as a rational expression of that original intuition, it relied heavily on Cartesian assumptions to derive anti-Cartesian conclusions. And this, it seems to me, is what is most helpful when we are trying to understand the deductions of the *Ethics*.

3. I owe my initial appreciation of the importance of this idea for Spinoza's philosophy to Stuart Hampshire, whose emphasis on it in his *Spinoza* (p. 47) was the inspiration for the interpretation offered in Curley (1).

4. Moore, p. 13. Moore does not offer this as a definition of metaphysics, but simply as a description of "the most important and interesting thing which philosophers have tried to do." But I think we can fairly take it as an account of what 17th-century Cartesians understood by metaphysics. A Kantian account, emphasizing that

metaphysics is a non-empirical science, seems to me anachronistic; e.g., I take the claim that there are bodies to be part of metaphysics for Descartes, but not one that he thought could be known by purely a priori means. As for Spinoza, though he *may* be committed to the possibility of an a priori proof of the existence of bodies, the way he in fact introduces them into his system is via an appeal to experience (IIA4).

5. This is the view of the piece-of-wax passage at the end of the Second Meditation (AT VII, 30), but not the view of the Synopsis which precedes the *Meditations* (AT VII, 14). I am taking the former view as dominant in Descartes, because it seems to me unclear what motivates the latter view. For more on this see the notes below.

6. Of course, at the time he was writing, Descartes' view was not common-sensical, as he was very much aware. Cf. AT VII, 440.

Perhaps Locke spoke for common sense when he insisted that solidity, as well as extension, was essential to bodies and that thought was not essential to minds, since the mind does not always think. But Locke has no good answer to the question: "What properties does the mind have when it is not thinking?" And it's not clear how far Locke and Descartes really differ on the essence of body. By solidity Locke seems to mean impenetrability, and it seems that Descartes would concede that impenetrability is a common property of bodies. Cf. *Essay* II, iv, 1, and K 238.

I take theism to be part of the common-sense view of the world, in the sense that a great many people, probably a majority in the West, would believe that the world was created by a personal being, not subject to human limitations, though many might concede that the existence of this being is not something we know with certainty.

7. For one reason, P5 plays a key role in Spinoza's deduction of P11, as will be evident to anyone who traces the deductive ancestry of P11.

8. Donagan ("Spinoza's Dualism") thinks it not so clear, but only because he thinks that in E IPP1-8 Spinoza is operating with "that sense of the word ["substance"] in which [Descartes] held that only God is a substance: namely that of a substance *quae nulla plane re indigeat*." And if "substance" is so understood, Descartes will not object to any of the first eight propositions. But I hope to show that Spinoza's proof of P5 does not depend on holding Descartes to this conception of substance.

9. Descartes shows some vacillation on the question of how many

material substances there are. The *Meditations* generally makes it appear that such ordinary items as stones (AT VII, 44) and pieces of wax (AT VII, 360) are material substances. But the Synopsis (AT VII, 14) suggests that there is only one material substance, body taken in general, and that other bodies are only modes of that substance. There indestructibility is essential to substances as such, and there is an interesting asymmetry between material substance and mental substance. There is a similar ambiguity in the *Principles.* Cf. II, 1, 23 (implying that there is only one material substance) with I, 60 (implying that each part of extended substance which can be defined by us in thought is itself an extended substance). Below we'll see at least one reason why Descartes might have been drawn toward the view that there is only one material substance. One reason I treat the Synopsis as not expressing Descartes' dominant view is that it seems to me that the derivation of Spinoza's philosophy from Descartes' is more interesting philosophically if Descartes is not made too much of a Spinozist to begin with.

10. I observe that Spinoza himself (TdIE §92, II / 34 / 10) glosses the notion of "existing in itself" as "being the cause of itself," and "existing in another" as "requiring a cause to exist."

Arguably, Descartes intends the formula cited in the text to apply only to God, so that if we use this formula to gloss Spinoza's definition of substance, we make Spinoza's proof that God is the only substance trivial. Cf. Donagan in "Spinoza's Dualism." But I take Descartes to intend the formula just quoted as a general one, covering both God and finite substances. It is only when he adds (in the following line) the qualifier *plane* (a substance is what *absolutely* needs no other thing) that Descartes says God is the only substance. I cannot see that Spinoza's argument for P5 depends on taking the definition this strictly and nothing in my reconstruction of the argument depends on this.

Leibniz identified an interesting difference between Descartes' formula and Spinoza's when he observed that Spinoza adds a condition not part of the common conception of substance: that substance must both exist in itself *and be conceived through itself.* For Descartes substance exists in itself, but is conceived through another. But I cannot see that Spinoza makes any use of this feature of the definition in his argument for P5. And in any case, he has an argument available for connecting the two features. Cf. Curley (1), pp. 14-16.

11. Most notably, Spinoza's formula brings in a reference to the

perceptions of the intellect, which has encouraged some interpreters to think the differences between the attributes are illusions of the finite intellect. This interpretation seems to be ruled out by E IIP7S, which suggests that the intellect in question is an infinite one, but puzzles remain. Bennett (§35.3) thinks that even though the intellect is infinite, it may be liable to illusion insofar as it perceives the attributes as basic. But this seems to me clearly unspinozistic.

It may be objected that Spinoza's definition of attribute is only superficially similar to Descartes' because Spinoza does not think that each substance has only one principal property, since he holds that the one substance has infinitely many attributes. I take it that his language in D4 and throughout the early propositions of Part I is deliberately unspecific on this point, because he recognizes the need to argue from common ground in order to be persuasive. Cf. TTP V, III / 76 / 30.

12. Though interpreters who think Spinoza does not identify substance and attribute ought to wonder what has happened to the attributes.

13. Cf. Bennett, p. 64. Bennett says "Spinoza clearly holds that there are *at least two* attributes, but only one substance" because he holds a theory about what Spinoza means by "infinite" according to which it would be consistent with God's having infinite attributes for God to have some finite number of attributes. Stated thus baldly, the theory may seem incredible, but many writers on Spinoza adopt it nowadays, so great is their aversion to the view that God has infinitely many unknown attributes. I find the correspondence with Tschirnhaus (specifically, Letters 63-66) unintelligible on their assumption.

Bennett makes his case for this interpretation of "infinite" in §19.1-2, pointing out that Spinoza regularly takes "infinite" to entail "all possible," and that his language frequently suggests that the entailment is an equivalence. I agree that "infinite" entails "all possible" for Spinoza, but think that any passage which suggests the converse entailment must be interpreted in such a way as to retain the opposition between "finite" and "infinite."

14. The clearest passage I know of comes from a work which cannot strictly be called a Cartesian text, *The Conversation with Burman* (see C, 17 = AT V, 156). Cottingham's commentary on an earlier passage (C, 15 = AT V, 155) makes clear the difficulties of giving a consistent account of Descartes' thought on this topic. If Spinoza

was familiar with the *Conversation*, it must have been in ms., since that work was not published until 1896.

15. My formulation here is indebted to Bennett's discussion, §16.4. But Bennett is there discussing certain passages in Spinoza, notably the explanation of "attribute" in Letter 9 (IV / 46 / 3), not anything in Descartes. For further Cartesian discussion of this topic, providing interesting confirmation of Bennett's reading, see the *Regulae* XIV (AT X, 443-444), and *Comments on a Certain Broadsheet*, AT VIIIB, 348-349 (Alquié III, 796-798). Arguably the passage cited in the text from the *Principles* falls short of my gloss on it, since it says only that we can't form a clear and distinct idea of substance apart from its principal attribute, not that we can form no conception of it at all. Garber calls attention to two other passages in which it seems to me that Descartes takes the stronger position: AT VII, 222, and *Principles* II, 9. Spinoza's exposition of Descartes suggests that this was the way *he* read Descartes. See PP IP7S (1 / 163 / 3-9).

16. I feel that the correctness of this reading of Spinoza is confirmed by Gueroult's agreement, 1, 48-50, 116-117. But I acknowledge that Spinoza does not always seem to have conceived things in this way. The *Short Treatise* seems at times to make more of a distinction than I think the mature Spinoza would. See, for example, KV I, 1st Dialogue, §9, 1 / 29 / 23-30 / 2. Other passages in the *Short Treatise* are more congenial to my interpretation. See, for example, KV I, vii, 10; 1 / 46 / 26-47 / 7.

17. See Loemker (ed.), Leibniz, *Philosophical Papers and Letters*, Reidel, 1976, pp. 198-199. Recently it is Bennett who has most forcefully pressed this objection. See §17.5.

18. It is a major theme of Gueroult's work (1, iii) that PP1-8 of Part I constitute Spinoza's theory of substances of one attribute. But though he considers Leibniz's objection (1, 120), he does not respond to it in this way. The reply suggested in the text is due to Bennett, who rejects it for the reasons indicated.

19. Actually, the question Descartes poses is whether the same wax still remains. But in the parallel passage in the *Principles* (II, 11) the question is whether the same body remains. That seems to me more accurate from Descartes' point of view. Alquié's annotation of this passage is, as usual, very valuable (II, 423-428). Here let me call attention particularly to his observation that it is not strictly correct, according to Descartes, that a body can change its size and remain

the same body. This is a consequence of the body's being identified with a portion of extension.

20. The wax passage helps to explain why Spinoza assumes that a substance's modes are accidental to it. Does the use I make of it commit the modal fallacy of which Bennett complains in §17.4, the mistake of inferring from "x and y are unalike only in respect of their accidental properties" to "x and y could become exactly alike?" I don't think so. The point is that, given the wax passage, it is difficult to see how Descartes could block the possibility that two finite material substances might come to be exactly alike as regards their intrinsic properties (counting all the properties mentioned in the wax passage as intrinsic). And the common-sense answer (that two bodies, identical as regards their intrinsic properties, might nevertheless be distinguished from one another by the extrinsic property of their relation to other bodies) is clearly circular.

21. In correspondence, Margaret Wilson points out that when Descartes identifies a body with the space it occupies, he draws a distinction between space (the portion of extension occupied by a body) and place (the external surface containing a body)—see *Principles* II, 10-14. So it might be suggested that the location in space which common sense takes to distinguish one body from another is, in these terms, its place, or relation to other bodies, not the space it is supposed to occupy. She adds, however, that "the relational theory [i.e., the theory which identifies a body's position with its relations to other bodies] also seems to give a reason why individuation of bodies must ultimately be prior to the determination of position."

22. See above, n. 9, for Descartes' vacillation on this point; for fuller discussion, see G. Rodis-Lewis, *L'individualité selon Descartes*.

23. Descartes certainly suggests that the question of individuation is resolved in essentially the same way for both bodies and minds in *Principles* I, 60. But insofar as the individuation of bodies is problematic, the parallel only suggests difficulties for the individuation of minds. In practice we individuate minds by the bodies with which they are united. Descartes' insistence that the mind is capable of existing apart from the body deprives us of that means, without supplying any good substitute.

24. Here I borrow from a recent article of mine, "Analysis in the *Meditations*: the Quest for Clear and Distinct Ideas," in Amélie Rorty's *Essays on Descartes' "Meditations,"* U of California Press, 1985. There I argue that the central difference between analysis and synthe-

sis in Descartes is that a synthetic work (paradigmatically, the "Geometric Exposition" following the Second Replies, but less clearly and consistently, the *Principles*) assumes possession of clear and distinct ideas, whereas an analytic work, like the *Meditations*, shows how to arrive at clear and distinct ideas through critical reflection on common-sense intuitions.

25. Descartes does not use the term "attribute" in this passage. But he does allow that God may have more than one attribute, even in that strict sense of the term in which an attribute is constitutive of the substance whose essence it is. Cf. *Comments on a Certain Broadsheet*, AT VIIIB, 348 (Alquié III, 797). For reasons obscure to me, Donagan (in "Spinoza's Dualism") seems to deny this.

26. Cf. the opening line of the Fifth Meditation.

27. This point seems to be recognized by Lachièze-Rey, pp. 42-43.

28. E.g., that there is nothing potential in his idea of God (AT VII, 47) or that God has the power of existing *per se* (AT VII, 50). That the definition should provide the basis for non-trivial deductions is important to Descartes as evidence that *this* idea of God is the idea of a "true and immutable nature," not a fiction. Bennett (§18.3) represents Descartes as defining God in a way Descartes would clearly reject. See Curley (2), p. 151, on Descartes' anticipation of "one Russellian criticism of Meinongian objects."

29. Cf. *Descartes' "Principles,"* IP7S (1 / 162 / 21), and *Metaphysical Thoughts*, II, x.

30. I infer this from the prominence in the *Short Treatise* of the theme to which Spinoza here draws attention. Cf. KV I, ii, 28-30; iii, n.a; v, 1; vi, 1; and vii, 1-2, 6-8. Spinoza is silent on this topic in the *Ethics*, perhaps because he could not raise it without engaging in a polemic he feared might be offensive.

31. It's interesting to note that in the *Metaphysical Thoughts*, where Spinoza, consistently with Descartes' conception of God, tries to explain God's omnipresence without attributing extension to him, he winds up claiming that God's omnipresence is one of those things which surpass man's understanding. Cf. CM II, iii (1 / 254 / 28) with Meyer's Preface (1 / 132 / 25). The question whether God's omnipresence requires us to conceive of him as extended is a major issue between Descartes and More in the correspondence which passed between them in late 1648 and 1649.

32. Perhaps because there would be a problem for Descartes in recognizing both thought and eternity as attributes of God, given his

doctrine that the divine attributes are inseparable. That would seem to entail that the only thinking things are eternal ones.

33. Cf. *Principles* I, 54, where the idea of God is identified as that of an uncreated and independent thinking substance.

34. In correspondence Margaret Wilson objects that "Descartes often speaks of something as the cause of something else, where there's no issue of the cause in itself entailing the effect in question. For instance, changes in the brain don't in themselves 'entail' mental states, but are sometimes said to cause them." Nevertheless, when Descartes is expounding his doctrine of continuous creation (AT VII, 49), he treats the fact that my present existence does not follow from my past existence as a reason why my past existence cannot explain my present existence, and a reason why we need to invoke the will of an omnipotent being as the cause of my present existence.

35. E.g., when Descartes states his fundamental causal principle in the Geometric Exposition—"A4: Whatever reality or perfection there is in a thing exists formally or eminently in its first and adequate cause"—the provision that the cause may contain the perfection of the effect eminently is presumably meant to allow for the possibility of an immaterial substance's creating material substances. Does Spinoza's gloss on the notion of eminent reality in his exposition of Descartes (I / 155 / 25) allow for that possibility? Cf. AT VII, 161.

36. We have here another potential explanation of the fact that in the Synopsis of the *Meditations* Descartes holds that there is only one extended substance and that indestructibility is a mark of substance. I am assuming Spinoza will allow that extension is divisible, so long as divisibility is not taken to entail separation into parts which are really distinct from one another. I think this is implicit in the passage in IP15s beginning at II / 59 / 32.

37. Bennett, p. 64.

38. This way of dealing with the problem was first suggested to me by various passages in Gueroult, vol. I, but I am not sure this represents Gueroult's final solution to the problem. It runs contrary to the answer Spinoza himself had suggested in KV I, ii, 17, insofar as it assumes that the attributes, conceived separately, do have a necessity of existing. The notes to §17 suggest to me that at that stage Spinoza was still struggling with the problem and that by the time he wrote the *Ethics* he may have reached a different solution.

39. Here we might appeal to Spinoza's paraphrase of P7 in P8D: "A substance of one attribute does not exist unless it is unique (P5),

and it pertains to its nature to exist (P7)." This applies P7 to substances of one attribute, which, I suggest, are not to be distinguished from that attribute.

40. The situation parallels the so-called paradoxes of strict implication in modal logic. If *p implies q* means *It is not possible that p & not-q*, then any necessary truth is implied by any proposition whatever and any two necessary propositions imply one another.

41. See Curley (1), pp. 4-28, 36-38, 74-77. Bennett (§23) characterizes my interpretation as radical and improbable partly because he thinks it implausible that Spinoza should radically revise the traditional concept of substance without making it clearer that he has done so. I feel somewhat confirmed in my view by the fact that Gueroult arrived at similar conclusions by a different route. See Gueroult I, i, 15, 21-22.

42. Cf. Bennett, §23.

43. See above, §§8 and 11. Let me emphasize, however, that this tendency in Descartes does not seem to stem from a strict construction of the definition of substance given in *Principles* I, 51. If it did, Descartes would have no justification at all for the asymmetry he insists on between minds and bodies in the passage that seems most explicitly to proclaim that there is only one material substance, the Synopsis to the *Meditations*.

44. Perhaps the best passages in support of this view are in the *Short Treatise* (KV II, xxii, 5; xx, 3, n.c). But it is also natural to read E IP15s in these terms. Bennett's exposition of the *real* basis for Spinoza's monism relies heavily on that scholium.

45. For more on this, see below, §14. For a summary statement of Descartes' adherence to this program, see *Principles* IV, 198. For Spinoza, see Letter 6, IV / 25 / 1-9. I put the terms "primary" and "secondary" in quotes because neither Descartes nor Spinoza uses this language, which is due to Boyle.

46. I raise this as a general question needing to be answered by anyone tempted to interpret modes as properties of substance, not as a question arising peculiarly from Bennett's interpretation, but of course I have Bennett very much in mind. I've discussed Bennett's interpretation of Spinoza's monism in much greater detail in a paper forthcoming in the proceedings of the Jerusalem Spinoza Conference of April 1987.

47. If I understand Bennett (§49.3), he does, in fact, allow that Spinoza's God can change, since IIL7s indicates that the whole of

nature persists through change (i.e., retains its numerical identity through change), and hence undergoes change. But we might rather take this as a reason for not identifying Spinoza's God with the whole of nature.

48. The Latin here rendered as "body of the whole universe" is *facies totius universi*. It is terribly difficult to know how to translate *facies*. (The OLD offers a long list of possibilities.) Spinoza does not tell us that the *facies* of the whole universe is supposed to be a mediate infinite mode of extension, and some have taken it to be a mode of both thought and extension. See Wolfson, I, 247. But when he introduces the term in Letter 64, Spinoza does refer us to IIL7S (= II/101/26-102/18), which suggests that he thinks of it as a mode of extension only and encourages the translation adopted in the text. The other main source of information about the infinite modes (KV I, ix) mentions only immediate infinite modes. For an interesting discussion see Gueroult, I, xi.

49. Not that there is no historical precedent at all for such a doctrine. As Gueroult notes (I, 309), Philo and the Neoplatonists had also inserted intermediaries between the infinite cause and its finite effects. So far as I can see, however, that parallel does not shed much light on the infinite modes in Spinoza.

50. Bennett is clear about this: "Spinoza attributes to the extended world something he calls 'motion and rest.' If this is asserted at his most basic metaphysical level, as it seems to be, he cannot mean by 'motion' and 'rest' what we mean by them. Only things in space can move; and at Spinoza's most basic metaphysical level there are no occupants, but only space, its different regions altering in orderly ways . . . Spinoza ought to use 'motion and rest' to mean something like 'those alterations in space which can be conceptualized, one level up, as movements of things in space" (§26).

51. Cf. Hampshire, pp. 44-45.

52. The assumption that Spinoza's God may be identified with the whole of Nature is so common in the Spinoza literature that few commentators feel any need to justify it. An interesting recent attempt occurs in Delahunty, ch. v, §1. But Delahunty curiously misreads Letter 43, attributing to Spinoza himself the claim that the universe is God, whereas Spinoza is in fact contending, against Velthuysen, that his having said that all things emanate necessarily from the nature of God does not commit him to holding that the

universe is God. I take this letter to be a clear rejection of that kind of pantheism.

There are other passages which would offer better support for this interpretation. I cited two from the *Short Treatise* above, in a note to §12. But these passages both come from an early and immature work, seem to have no parallel in the *Ethics*, and are inconsistent with other passages in the KV (e.g., I, viii) and in the TdIE (§76). For discussion, see Curley (1), p. 42. I think the general disposition to identify Spinoza's God with the whole of Nature comes mainly from what I argue in the text to be a misreading of the Preface to E IV.

53. This reading of the phrase *Deus seu Natura* may already be found in Lachièze-Rey, p. 51, who calls attention to KV I, viii, and Letter 73. There is an analogy here between Spinoza and Aristotle. Readers of Book Zeta of the *Metaphysics* may well be surprised to find that when Aristotle asks, "What is substance?" he apparently rejects the claims of matter and the concrete thing which is a compound of form and matter (1029a26-33) in favor of the form, "by reason of which the matter is some definite thing" (1041b8). I do not mean to suggest any direct influence, only that we should not expect the answer to "What is substance?" to be obvious.

Garrett, in correspondence, agrees that for Spinoza God is *natura naturans*, but adds that there is still not a Cartesian "real distinction" between *natura naturans* and *natura naturata*.

54. I have discussed these problems in detail in "Descartes on the Creation of the Eternal Truths," *Philosophical Review*, 93(1984):569-597 (followed by a page of typographical corrections in the next issue).

55. Cf. Meyer's Preface to *Descartes' "Principles,"* 1 / 132 / 25.

56. That this is not an implausible way for a philosopher influenced by Descartes to understand the concept of nature is illustrated by Malebranche, who writes: "Nature is nothing but the general laws which God has established in order to construct or to preserve his work by the simplest means, by an action which is always uniform, constant, perfectly worthy of an infinite wisdom and of a universal cause." *Traité de la nature et de la grace, Oeuvres* v, 148. Malebranche may be influenced here by the Sixth Meditation, AT VII, 80.

57. In the language of the *Short Treatise*, they are incorruptible, not through their own power, but only through the power of their cause. Cf. KV II, v, 5, 9.

58. Or are corruptible, to use once again the language of KV II, v, 5.

59. As I believe Spinoza also recognizes in §§99-103 of the TdIE, and in KV I, 2nd Dialogue, §10. I have argued more fully for the interpretation advanced in this section in Curley (1), pp. 66-78.

60. Commentators on Spinoza have frequently complained that Spinoza never carries out the deduction of the finite from the infinite which his system (e.g., in IP16) would seem to require to be possible. In my view a proper understanding of IP28 requires us to see that he would regard such a deduction as impossible even for an infinite intellect. Bennett seems to accept this reading (§27), though he is more disposed than I would be to see Spinoza as torn by conflicting commitments (§§28-29). Gueroult also seems to arrive at a similar reading (I, xii, 11), though I am not sure that he goes as far as I would. E.g., as I understand his interpretation of the mediate infinite mode, it "contains" the infinite series of finite things. If that is right, it seems to me to lead to trouble, since the mediate infinite mode follows from the absolute nature of the attribute, as Spinoza makes quite clear in IP23D.

61. Cf. Bennett §28.1, and Curley (1), 101-106. Delahunty (pp. 163-165) also seems to think Spinoza is more ambivalent on this issue than I do. I conjecture that if we could put to Spinoza the question "Is this world the only possible world?" his initial instinct would be to answer yes, but that discussion of his systematic commitments might lead him in the end to make a distinction between a sense in which it is ("Given the prior history of this world, and given the necessary laws operating in it, there is only one possible future for this world") and a sense in which it is not ("Given the laws of nature alone, there is a plurality of possible histories by which they might have been instantiated"). I agree with Bennett (§29.7) that Spinoza never squarely faced this issue. But I don't think his commitment to explanatory rationalism was so strong that he could not have accepted this result.

CHAPTER II

1. For discussion of the doctrine of complete and incomplete substances, see the Fourth Replies (AT VII, 222). For discussion of the doctrine of substantial union, see the correspondence with Regius

(December 1641, January 1642) and Elisabeth (21 May 1643, 28 June 1643), K 121-122, 127-128, 130, 137-141.

2. Here I rely on an interpretation of Descartes argued at greater length in Curley (2), ch. 4.

3. Cf. Meditation Six, AT VII, 78, noting particularly the emphasis added in the French version at the end of the argument for the real distinction. For similar identifications, see AT VII, 63 ("to the nature of myself, or [sive] my mind"), 73 ("of my own essence, that is, of the essence of my mind"). The identification of the self with the soul was theologically sensitive, as is evident from the correspondence with Regius (December 1641, January 1642, Kenny, 121-122, 126-130). Aquinas rejects the Platonic doctrine that a man is a soul using a body, and hence, a being per accidens, in SCG II, 57, and ST I, 75, 4, citing Augustine (City of God, XIX, 3) as being in agreement. (It's not clear that Augustine does agree with Aquinas in this. The passage cited is a report of Varro's views, which Augustine goes on to criticize. In On the Morals of the Catholic Church, ch. 27, Augustine's view seems to be Platonic.) I take it that the identification of the man with the soul is at least a strong tendency in Platonism. Even if the Alcibiades (129-130) is not genuine, it seems implicit in the Phaedo (62b, 82e). Cf. Plotinus, Enneads I, i. Although a Platonic account of man as a soul using a body might seem more congenial to the Christian doctrine of immortality, the Aristotelian account is more congenial to the doctrine of the resurrection of the body. Cf. Aquinas, SCG IV, lxxix, 10.

4. Aquinas attributes this metaphor to Plato, though it doesn't seem to occur explicitly in the Alcibiades. Arguably it is implicit in the craft analogies Socrates does use there. But those analogies also imply that the soul must have a body fit for the use the soul makes of it (cf. Aristotle, De anima, 407b14-26), which seems contrary to the Phaedo's view that the body is the prison of the soul. The first explicit occurrence of the pilot-ship metaphor seems to be in De anima 413a8, where Aristotle abstains from committing himself on its appropriateness. Plotinus (Enneads IV, iii, 21) finds the analogy good in some respects, but contends that "none of the ways of a thing's being in anything which are currently spoken of fits the relation of soul to body." Descartes likens the relationship of soul to body to that of craftsman to tool in the Fifth Replies (AT VII, 354), but if what I argue in the text is correct, this runs contrary to the intuitions the doctrine of substantial union was meant to express.

5. Letter of 10 June 1643, AT III, 684.

6. See the letters to Elisabeth of 21 May 1643 and 28 June 1643, helpfully annotated in Alquié III, 18-23, 43-48.

7. Cf. PA §30, AT XI, 351 (Alquié III, 976), with Aquinas, SCG II, 72.

8. Not that Spinoza did not share the intuitions of those who found interaction unintelligible. Cf. E IPP2,3, and their ancestors in AA4,5 of App I of the *Short Treatise*. But it's worth bearing in mind that in the *Short Treatise*, even though he has arrived at the conception of the soul as the idea of the body (e.g., in KV II, Pref, I / 51 / 32), and even though he finds full interaction between mind and body unacceptable, Spinoza does accept a limited interaction. Cf. II, xix-xx. (For an attempt to explain these passages away, see Deleuze, p. 94. I don't find the explanation persuasive. The language Deleuze appeals to, to show that Spinoza does not really accept interaction there, is precisely the kind of language Descartes used to show how interaction was possible.)

9. But not trivially, since Spinoza requires at least two intervening propositions to get from one statement to the other: P11 and P13.

10. Cf. Meyer's preface to *Descartes' "Principles,"* I / 132.

11. Cf. the TdIE §§21-22: "After we clearly perceive that we feel such a body, and no other, then . . . we infer clearly that the soul is united to the body, which union is the cause of such a sensation, but we cannot understand what that sensation and union are; . . . when . . . I know the essence of the soul, I know that it is united to the body." The TdIE contains no account of the essence of the soul. The KV, which does contain an account (I / 51 / 32, 91 / 29, 101 / 23, 119 / 6), limits itself to maintaining that the soul is the idea in the thinking thing (i.e., in God) of the body. So far as I can see, neither of these works explicitly contains the doctrine of the *Ethics*, that mind and body are one and the same thing, conceived under different attributes.

12. Cf. KV II, Pref, §3, I / 53 / 3.

13. Bennett says (§34.3) that the *sic* in II / 90 / 8 is comparative rather than inferential and my own translation rather suggests that, though perhaps not as unambiguously as Bennett's does. Nevertheless, I'm inclined to believe that it does have some inferential force. I think Spinoza does believe that the identity of the thinking substance and the extended substance makes it reasonable for us to expect to

find an analogous identity among the modes of thought and the modes of extension.

14. These questions are all implicit in Bennett, §34.3, though he does not put them in quite the way I do. I do not in fact accept all the presuppositions of these questions, since I do not attribute to Spinoza a doctrine of parallelism in the sense in which Bennett understands it in §31. (But cf. §37.1.) For more on this, see below.

15. See Bennett, §31.2-5. Delahunty (p. 198) notes the oddity of the demonstration, but I don't find his explanation at all helpful. Gueroult's account of the demonstration (II, iv, 10) does not seem sensitive to the difficulties.

16. As Bennett rightly argues, §31.6.

17. Bennett, commenting on an earlier version of this ms., finds my treatment of the unknown attributes "over-bold . . . the reader is entitled to be reminded that the *Ethics* says nothing at all about unknown attributes." But Tschirnhaus, who seems not to have understood Spinoza's concept of infinity as Bennett does, took the *Ethics* to be committed to such attributes, and Spinoza never challenged his interpretation. Their correspondence (see Letters 63-66) seems unintelligible except on the assumption that there are infinitely many attributes which we cannot know because our mind is essentially the idea of a mode of extension. The ideas in thought of the modes of the unknown attributes are the minds or souls of those modes. I take it that this was Spinoza's view at least from the time of the *Short Treatise* (KV App. 2, §§9 and 12), and that he intended the *Ethics* to be so understood. I think he would have regarded this view as being implicit in IIP3 (in conjunction with IP16). It comes nearest to being explicit in IIP6C. Gueroult (II, iii, 2) takes it to be implicit in IIP1S.

18. For discussion, see Bennett, §§29.2 and 31.6. I'm not sure I accept Bennett's criticism of the argument Spinoza does offer, but I'm not attracted by that argument sufficiently to want to explain or defend it.

19. In §31.6, par. 4, Bennett briefly describes and abruptly dismisses an argument which seems to me to have more importance than he allows. Variations of this argument occur in three passages in the *Short Treatise*. See KV II, Pref, the note Gebhardt attaches to §2, beginning at I / 51 / 16; II, xx, the note Gebhardt attaches to §3, beginning at I / 97 / 29; and finally, App II, I / 117 / 14-29. Both notes are quite long and occur in the ms. without any explicit indication of the passage they are meant to annotate, so that their placement is a

matter of conjecture. I suspect this indicates that they, like the second appendix, are later than the main body of the text. There does not seem to be any comparable argument in the main body of the text. If that is correct, then these passages provide us, as it were, with a time-lapse photograph of the development of Spinoza's thought on this topic. It is on these passages that I rely for my explanation of IIP3.

20. Spinoza may not have been responsible for that paraphrase (cf. the *Collected Works*, I, 448, n. I.), but it seems to me quite in his spirit to assume the existence of many thinking things. I gather that Willis Doney ("Spinoza on Philosophical Skepticism" in Mandelbaum and Freeman) would say that at least in his earlier works Spinoza took skepticism seriously. But Spinoza's various jibes against the skeptic in the TdIE (e.g., §§47-48) suggest to me that even then Spinoza did not think the skeptic himself was serious about his skepticism.

21. Bennett observes (§30.1) that none of the Part II axioms is explicitly cited in the demonstrations of any of the first nine propositions in Part II. But I take IIP1D to depend tacitly on IIA2. Otherwise there is no justification for the reference to singular thoughts in the first step of the demonstration.

22. Spinoza says that the demonstration of IIP2 proceeds in the same way as that of IIP1. In the preceding note I argued that P1D makes tacit use of IIA2. If that's right, we must see something analogous in P2D.

23. The Latin text of A4 refers simply to "a certain body." The NS version refers to "our body." Whether that translation had Spinoza's authorization or not, I feel certain it is a helpful gloss. Officially Spinoza does not prove that the human body exists until IIP13, and then he does so by way, not only of A4, but also of P11. Nevertheless, I think P2D has to assume, on the basis of A4, the existence of *some* body.

24. I am assuming that an idea of a mode of extension will affirm the existence of its object. I think Spinoza would assume this and that, arguably, Descartes would too. See "Descartes, Spinoza and the Ethics of Belief," in Mandelbaum and Freeman.

25. I would argue also that it speaks in favor of this account of the doctrine of parallelism that it makes it readily intelligible that Spinoza should think that there would be distinct modes of thought corresponding to the modes of the unknown attributes. If the doctrine

of parallelism were motivated primarily by the desire to explain away the appearance of interaction between mind and body, as in Bennett's account, it is hard to understand why thought should be so extensive.

26. Bennett, §34.2. Bennett thinks he can explain why Spinoza affirms this identity, but I find his explanation (§§34-36) incredible. I cannot see Spinoza granting the existence of trans-attribute differentiae which cannot be grasped by any intellect. This is partly because I think he would refuse to recognize the existence of any properties inconceivable to the intellect, and partly because I think the more specific properties which distinguish, say, one mode of extension from another must be properties which presuppose extension.

27. KV App II, 1 / 118 / 31. Cf. TdIE §33.

28. KV II, xx, 3, n.c, 1 / 97 / 25. This passage seems to me to come closer to the doctrine of the *Ethics* than anything else in the *Short Treatise*. Like the passage cited in the preceding paragraph, it comes from one of the three passages referred to above in n. 19. It seems likely that all three are later than the main body of the text of the KV, but we cannot really be more precise about their dating than that. Analogously, the nearest approach in the TdIE to the identity doctrine of the *Ethics* occurs in fn. f (§21), when Spinoza writes that those who do not conceive the soul through its true essence will imagine that what is in itself one is many. But this remark, while it may well be intended as a criticism of Descartes, is not so pointedly a rejection of the Cartesian doctrine as, say, E IIP21S. Since it occurs in a footnote, it is quite possibly later than the main text.

29. Although the formula from IIP21S is more restricted than that of IIP7S, it is interesting that when Spinoza cites IIP7S at the beginning of IIIP2S (II / 141 / 24) his paraphrase is actually much closer to IIP21S.

30. IIP11C, we should note, states a conclusion Spinoza had reached in his very earliest writings. Cf. TdIE §73, KV II, Pref.

31. There may be some argument about this. Bennett (§33.6) comments on our passage: "But that is said about individuals, not about all particular things. Spinoza may confine the term 'individual' [and hence, the term 'animate'] to organisms; certainly he does not extend it to physical items that do not have a fair degree of organic complexity." Similarly, Gueroult (II, 165) restricts the scope of our passage to composite bodies. This seems to be based partly on taking the definition at II / 99 / 26 to establish a special sense of the term "individual" which has to be read back into P13S. But I take IID7 to show

that Spinoza treats "individual" and "singular thing" as synonyms; the definition at II / 99 / 26 simply explains in more detail what individuality consists in for composite bodies. As Gueroult recognizes, taking "individual" to have a restricted scope is not sufficient to lessen the paradox in P13S. We must also take "thing" (both there and in P3) to have a special restricted meaning. That seems to me to rob restricted interpretations of their plausibility.

32. In Curley (1), pp. 126ff.

33. Cf. Margaret Wilson, "Objects, Ideas and Minds," in Kennington.

34. And I take VP39S to show that Spinoza recognized, what ought to be obvious enough from experience: that different people possess self-consciousness (which I presume includes conscious awareness of the state of one's body) in very different degrees, and that no human has full self-consciousness.

35. This is suggested by Bennett, §44.7.

36. The key passage is not in the *Ethics*, but in the *Metaphysical Thoughts*, II, vi. Though this work is nominally an (appendix to an) exposition of the Cartesian philosophy, I believe that, read carefully, it offers many useful clues as to Spinoza's own views. See my preface to it and *Descartes' "Principles"* in *The Collected Works of Spinoza*, vol. I. The passage in question is an interesting mix of Cartesian doctrines with doctrines peculiar to Spinoza.

37. I agree, then, with many of the things Bennett says about Spinoza's panpsychism in §33, though not with the restriction he places on the scope of the term "individual," and not with the use he makes of Nagel's article on panpsychism in *Mortal Questions*. In comments on an earlier version of this ms., Bennett (echoing §33.6) writes: "I don't see how, on this account of 'All things are animate,' Spinoza could say (as he does) that animatedness is a matter of degree. 3p6 isn't about a matter of degree." But I take it that, although the striving to persevere is common to all things, the power or force which things manifest in this striving *is* a matter of degree. Some things are better able than others to survive interaction with their environment while preserving their identity. The physical excursus which comes after IIP13S relates the varying degrees of this capacity to varying degrees in the physical complexity of the organism. If I understand Deleuze (p. 191) correctly, he intends something similar.

38. I'm thinking here primarily of Donagan. Bennett talks a good deal about Spinoza's dualism, but what he understands by that talk

(concept dualism, in the sense explained in the Preface, n. 5) seems a doctrine we should not deny to Spinoza. The main objection I have to Bennett's account at this point is that, insofar as he gives dualism a role to play in Spinoza's argument for parallelism, he seems to attribute more systematic importance to it than I think it has. I also think he's wrong to suggest that the doctrine of parallelism is, in the long run, more important than the doctrine of mind-body identity (§36.3). And I find his explanation of the mind-body identity extremely implausible. See above, n. 26.

Donagan, on the other hand, seems to think that Spinoza's monism about substance (which Bennett cheerfully allows) is spurious. Otherwise I cannot understand his talk about a "professed monism" or his comparison of Spinoza's monism about substance with Descartes' nominal geocentrism. I think this comes largely from his taking seriously a problem which Bennett (so far as I can see) does not regard as serious: how can one substance have two (or more) attributes when an attribute is understood to constitute the essence of the substance to which it belongs? Donagan concentrates primarily on the relation between substance and its attributes, but I assume that he would raise analogous difficulties about the identity Spinoza claims to exist between modes of extension and their ideas.

39. Cf. Letter 64 (to Schuller): "The essence of the mind (by IIP13) consists in this alone, that it is the idea of an actually existing body."

40. Cf. E IIL1 with KV II, Pref, 1 / 51 / 16-52 / 33.

41. Cf. KV II, Pref, 1 / 52 / 20: "To produce in substantial thought an Idea, knowledge, mode of thinking, such as [this soul of] ours now is, not just any body whatever is required (for then it would have to be known differently than it is), but one which has this proportion of motion and rest and no other. *For as the body is, so is the soul, Idea, knowledge, etc.*" (my emphasis). Cf. also KV App II, 3: "To understand now what this mode is, which we call soul, *how it has its origin from the body, and how also its change depends on the body*, which I maintain to be the union of soul and body, we must first note . . ." (1 / 117 / 14, my emphasis).

42. In Spinoza's usage, "imagination" includes ordinary sense perception, but also includes what we would normally call imagination.

43. Recent writers on the mind-body problem in Spinoza seem particularly anxious to free Spinoza of any taint of "reductive" materialism. Cf. Wallace Matson, "Spinoza's Theory of Mind," p. 53, and Douglas Odegard, "The Body Identical with the Human Mind: A

Problem in Spinoza's Philosophy," p. 65 (both in Mandelbaum and Freeman). If the rejection of reductive materialism means only that Spinoza does not deny the existence of minds (as it seems to in Odegard) or that the mind cannot be defined solely in terms of modes of extension (as it seems to in Matson), then there can be no objection. But if it means that understanding the nature and properties of the mind does not require you to understand the nature and properties of the body which is its object, then I think it needs more argument than it gets. Note that when Matson tries to support textually his claim that Spinoza was not a reductive materialist, he appeals to passages from the TdIE (§§ 58, 68, II / 22, 26) and the KV (II, Pref, I / 51 / 18; App II, I / 118 / 31), without considering the possibility that Spinoza's view may have changed by the time he wrote the *Ethics*. Some of these passages assert nothing more than a conceptual distinction between mind and body, i.e., affirm that aspect of Cartesianism which Spinoza never gave up. But the one passage which affirms a real distinction between mind and body (I / 118 / 31) seems to me to represent a view Spinoza was in the process of giving up even as he wrote the KV. See above, §7.

I think writers on this topic need to be more sensitive to the immaturity of the KV. Although Spinoza already has there the doctrine that the mind is the idea of the body, and even proclaims that the soul has its origin from the body (I / 117 / 15), nowhere in that work does he adopt the formula of E IIP21S, that the mind and the body are one and the same thing, considered in two different ways. I suggest that he came to see this latter formula as providing a metaphysical explanation, not only of the mind's awareness of and concern for the body, but also of its dependence on the body for its knowledge of other things.

44. Bennett acknowledges (he would say: insists on) the fact that the order of understanding proceeds from body to mind and not conversely. See particularly §30.2, but also the various index entries under "physical, explanatory primacy of." Perhaps the reason why he does not regard this as a desertion of dualism is that he thinks this order of explanation is imposed on us only because (as Bennett reads Spinoza) we know relatively little about the operations of the mind and much more about the operations of the body. Cf. §§51.6 and 75.4. But I don't think that was Spinoza's view. I think he took Part III to establish psychology as a science on a par with the physics of his time.

45. See, for example, Gilbert Ryle, *The Concept of Mind*, ch. i.

46. See, particularly, VP20S (II / 294 / 17-24), P40S.

47. Subject, of course, to the qualifications noted above in §6.

48. So I am still inclined toward the "symmetrical" account of the eternity doctrine which I expounded in Curley (1), pp. 137-143, and which Bennett criticizes in §82.3. One reason I don't find his alternative account more appealing is that it seems to rely on the doctrine of trans-attribute differentiae, which I think cannot be right. See above, n. 26. To the extent that the "something of the mind" which is eternal is its essence (as P23D suggests), Spinoza has some justification for his doctrine, but an equally good justification for holding that something of the body is eternal. To the extent that Spinoza wants to identify that something with the intellect (as he apparently does in P29—cf. P40C), I think he has no justification for it. I'm encouraged in this reading by the fact that Gueroult too seems to have committed himself to a symmetrical reading of the doctrine of the eternity of the mind (II, v, 21).

CHAPTER III

1. The quote derives from John Aubrey's *Brief Lives*, ed. A. Clark, Clarendon Press, 1898, I, 357.

2. The most important Cartesian texts in connection with this part of Descartes' philosophy are given in CSM and K. In K see particularly the correspondence with Princess Elisabeth and Chanut. There is also relevant material (a wider selection of Descartes' own letters, and the letters addressed to him by his correspondents) in Blom.

3. So the title is translated by John Basore in the Loeb Library edition of Seneca's *Moral Essays* (Harvard UP, 1979, vol. II). In his letter of 4 August 1645 Descartes complains that to translate *vivere beate* into French by *vivre heureusement* would be misleading. He takes it that good fortune is both necessary and sufficient for *heur*, whereas it is neither necessary nor sufficient for the *vita beata* which Seneca has in mind. So he proposes to translate *vivere beate* by *vivre en béatitude*, understood as a life consisting in a perfect contentment of mind and interior satisfaction. I think the English *happiness* is apt to have the same connotations of good luck as *heur*. The relation between happiness and good fortune seems to have already been much discussed when Aristotle wrote. Cf. NE 1096a1-4.

4. K 180. Cf. Cicero, *De finibus* III, vii, xiii. Alquié, in annotating

Descartes' claim (PA §1) that the teachings of the ancients regarding the passions of the soul are "for the most part so implausible," says that Descartes undoubtedly has in mind the Stoic teaching that the wise man can be happy even on the rack. But Descartes affirms that Stoic teaching not only in the correspondence with Elisabeth, but also in PA §148.

5. Elisabeth to Descartes, 13 September 1645, AT IV, 289-90, Blom, p. 149.

6. Note the limitations of this claim. I would not construe it as an affirmation of his total independence of his predecessors, as Rodis-Lewis and Alquié seem to do. Cf. Rodis-Lewis, p. 29, with Alquié III, 942, 951. Rodis-Lewis' introduction contains a very interesting sketch of the relation of Descartes' psychology to those of his predecessors, but it would have been perfectly consistent with the claim cited in the text (though perhaps not consistent with Descartes' temperament) for him to acknowledge the influence of Vives, the predecessor who seems to come closest to him.

7. See Alquié III, 1005n, and also his comment on §173 at III, 1081n. I simplify by taking Platonic psychology to be defined by the theory elaborated in Book IV of the *Republic*, and I make no attempt to explore the changes that doctrine went through in the Aristotelian tradition. But it should be noted here that in the *Phaedo* Plato had adopted what we might anachronistically call a more Cartesian theory, treating conflicts of desire as conflicts between body and soul (94c). It seems reasonable to suppose that this fact is connected with his deploying in that work an argument for immortality based on the simplicity of the soul (78b-80b).

8. Here Descartes does claim more originality than is his due. See Rodis-Lewis, pp. 24-27.

9. Rodis-Lewis (pp. 21-22) finds an example in the *Summa philosophica* of Eustachius of Saint Paul, who lists love, hate, desire, aversion, joy and sadness as concupiscible appetites, and hope, despair, boldness, fear and anger as irascible appetites. But no doubt the division goes back, as CSM suggests, to Book IV of the *Republic*.

10. In a letter to Chanut (1 November 1646) Descartes is more guarded: "In examining [the passions] I have found them almost all good, and so useful in this life that our soul would have no reason to want to remain joined to this body for a moment, if it could not feel them." For the claim that the Stoic wise man is always free of the passions, see Cicero, *De finibus* III, x.

11. Rodis-Lewis notes (p. 218, n.2) that Descartes had always been opposed to the insensibility of the Stoic sage, citing passages as early as the *Discourse* (AT VI, 8) and as late as a letter to Silhon of 1648 (AT V, 135). Cf. also the letter to Elisabeth of 1 September 1645 (K 167-171).

12. *Générosité* is a 17th-century French version of Aristotle's *megalopsychia*, a Greek term equally difficult to get into English without being misleading. The revised Oxford translation (*The Complete Works of Aristotle*, ed. Jonathan Barnes, Princeton: Princeton UP, 1984, 2 vols.) uses *pride* in the *Nicomachean Ethics* (IV, iii) and *magnanimity* in the *Eudemian Ethics* (III, v). If *magnanimity* is taken in its etymological sense, *great-souled*, it seems the happier choice. Descartes recognizes the ancestry of his *générosité* when he relates it to the *magnanimitas* of the scholastic philosophers in §161.

13. The Descartes of the PA does recognize the existence of intellectual love and joy in various places (e.g., §§79, 91, 139, and 147), but the account of these emotions and of their relation to their sensual counterparts in the treatise is certainly less detailed (and arguably less clear) than it is in the letter to Chanut of 1 February 1647, where the list of intellectual emotions also includes sadness and desire. See Alquié's annotation of the passages cited.

14. Descartes distinguishes three species of love: affection, friendship and devotion, felt, respectively, for those one considers inferior to oneself, those one considers one's equals, and those one considers one's superiors. Affection may be felt for plants and the lower animals, in which case we always prefer our own interests to those of the thing loved. Devotion may be felt for God, one's prince, one's country, one's city, and even for a particular person. Where the love is devotion, we willingly sacrifice our own interests, even our lives, for the sake of the thing loved. All of this is presented descriptively, but I think it is intended prescriptively. But what of friendship? There is no man so imperfect that the truly noble man will not feel friendship for him when he feels that that man loves him. But how will, or should, we act towards a friend? Descartes is silent on this point in the PA, though elsewhere he contends that a true friend will be prepared to sacrifice himself for his friend. Cf. the letter to Chanut of 1 February 1647 (Alquié III, 719, followed by interesting annotation on 720).

15. E.g., "Emotions . . . are called *perturbations* [of the mind] because they frequently obstruct right reasoning . . . [in] that they mil-

itate against the real good and in favor of the apparent and most immediate good . . . [A]lthough the real good must be sought in the long term, which is the job of reason, appetite seizeth upon a present good without foreseeing the greater evils that necessarily attach to it" (*DH* xii, 1).

16. This account is drawn eclectically from three sources: *EL* I, vii; *Lev* I, vi; and *DH* xi-xii.

17. Kavka (pp. 11-12) offers a number of criticisms, the most serious of which is that "deliberation consists not of alternating desires and aversions to perform an act, but of cumulative consideration of reasons for and against performing an act." But I think Hobbes acknowledges the cumulative element when he writes that "deliberation is nothing else but a weighing, as it were in scales, the conveniences and inconveniences of the fact we are attempting; where that which is more weighty doth necessarily, according to its inclination, prevail with us" (*DC* xiii, 16).

18. *DH* xi, 4. Cf. *Lev* vi, 7: "Whatsoever is the object of any man's appetite, that is it which he for his part calleth *good*."

19. See, most notably, Bernard Gert, in his introduction to *Man and Citizen*, and F. S. McNeilly, *The Anatomy of Leviathan*, Macmillan, 1968.

20. For other examples, see *DC* iii, 21; v, i; vi, 4; *Lev* xi, 1-2; xv, 16, 31; xxvii, 8, in addition to various passages cited below.

21. I think the best way to read Hobbes is as holding what Kavka (p. 64) calls predominant egoism, defined by the theses that (i) for most people in most situations the "altruistic gain / personal loss" ratio needed to reliably motivate self-sacrificing actions is large; and (ii) the scope of altruistic motives strong enough to normally override self-interest is, for most people, confined to family, close friends or associates, or particular groups or projects to which the individual is devoted. (I omit two further theses which seem implicit in Kavka's first claim.) Kavka does not attribute this view to Hobbes himself, but he might well have. Not only does it reconcile a prima facie contradiction in Hobbes, but some passages (e.g., *Lev* xix, 4) seem to me to come as close to stating it as we could expect. And it does seem sufficient for Hobbes' political argument.

22. So, e.g., *conatus* is the term Hobbes uses for "endeavor" in the Latin translation of *Lev* vi, 1-2.

23. I gather from §54.2 that Bennett takes IIIP6 to apply only to individuals, where "individual" is understood as applying only to the

complex bodies described in the definition at II / 99-100. But this involves equating *res* with *individuum* in that rather special sense, and I don't see any warrant for doing that. The *Short Treatise* supports the view that the doctrine of the *conatus* applies quite generally, since it states the doctrine without any qualification (KV I, v, I) and does not have any special theory of what constitutes an individual which could be read into the doctrine.

24. Letter 58 (IV / 266 / 13ff) seems clear enough evidence of that. Cf. Matheron, p. 65.

25. I am, then, interpreting P6 as a teleological doctrine, in the sense in which Bennett explains the concept of teleology in §57.4, i.e., as a doctrine which has, roughly, the form "If it would help him, he will do it." One powerful argument in favor of this reading, I think, is the fact to which Bennett calls attention in §57.5, that if the doctrine is interpreted non-teleologically, it is very difficult to understand the force of the clause "as far as it can." I do not interpret P6 as being teleological in the stronger sense which Bennett calls "teleological-cognitive" (§68.3), i.e., as having the form "If he thinks it would help him, he will do it," because I think Spinoza intends the doctrine to apply to things which are not capable of having thoughts about the future.

As I read Bennett, he thinks Spinoza *intended* P6 only as a non-teleological doctrine, which would have the form "If he does it, it will help him." But he also thinks that immediately after P6 Spinoza illicitly treated it as if it were a teleological doctrine, and indeed, that at least by P28 he takes himself to have established a teleological-cognitive doctrine. Part of the reason for Bennett's construing P6 in this way is that he reads the Appendix to Part I as committed to a denial of all teleology, both cosmic and human. I have criticized his reading of that Appendix in a forthcoming article, "Bennett on Spinoza on teleology." But part of his reason for this construal of P6 is that he thinks the only way we can understand Spinoza to have a tolerable argument for P6 is if we take him to be construing it in a non-teleological way. I reply to that in the text. I agree with Bennett that P28 is a telelogical-cognitive doctrine, which does not follow from the *conatus* doctrine, conceived simply as a teleological doctrine. Not only does it not follow from the *conatus* doctrine, but given the uncontroversial assumption that we sometimes mistake our interests, it is inconsistent with the *conatus* principle, since the two principles yield incompatible predictions in cases of such error.

26. A fact stressed both by Wallace Matson and Bennett, §55.1.

27. Bennett (§57) suggests that Spinoza's paraphrase of P5 in P6D involves an illicit transition from "If things can destroy one another, they must have at least some incompatible properties" to "If things can destroy one another, each must exert itself against the other."

28. The argument just sketched is similar to the one Bennett outlines at the end of §57.3, except that my argument reaches a conclusion which, in his terms, is teleological, whereas his argument reaches a non-teleological conclusion.

29. Matson seems to find it so; Bennett (§56) does not. Hobbes holds an analogous view in his *Dialogue of the Common Laws, English Works* VI, 88.

30. See Matson, pp. 407-408. Matson appeals to a difficult passage in the TdIE §57, where Spinoza seems to say that if we suppose a candle to be burning where there are no surrounding bodies, we must infer that it has no cause for its destruction, and that the candle and its flame would remain immutable. Part of the difficulty of the passage is that Spinoza gives this as an example of a hypothesis involving an impossible supposition, and it's unclear what he thinks the status of conditionals with impossible antecedents is. In the specific passage Matson appeals to, Spinoza seems to say that this particular conditional is true. But some scholars have suggested that the text must be corrupt, since Spinoza's usual view in the *Treatise* seems to be that we cannot make hypotheses about impossible situations. See *The Collected Works*, I, 26, n. 44, and TdIE §53. On the other hand, in the *Ethics* Spinoza does seem willing to assert conditionals with impossible antecedents (IVP68, P4D).

Matson recognizes that on his reading of this passage Spinoza is making a quite extraordinary claim. It is not surprising that living before Lavoisier, Spinoza should not have understood the role of oxygen in combustion. But it is surprising that he should apparently think that fire requires no fuel whatever to maintain itself. So Matson constructs on Spinoza's behalf a theory of fire according to which that would be true. Here it seems relevant to point out that Descartes' treatment of fire in the *Principles* (IV, 80-132) takes the fact that fire requires fuel as one of the data which a satisfactory theory of fire must explain (§83). And the correspondence with Boyle makes it appear that Spinoza accepted the Cartesian theory of fire. Cf. Letter 11, IV/49/24, and the other entries under *ignis* in the Glossary-Index of the *Collected Works*.

31. The theory of definition is given in the TdIE §§92-97. I am indebted to Matheron (pp. 11-12) for the suggestion that we must seek the key to understanding this part of the *Ethics* in that unpublished work. For the record I note two facts: that Spinoza's theory of definition seems to reflect the influence of Hobbes' *De Corpore* I, i, 5; and that this same passage in Hobbes also seems to contain an explanation of Spinoza's 1A4, an axiom which Spinoza scholars have sometimes found very puzzling.

32. This seems clearer, actually, in the corresponding passage in the *Short Treatise*, I / 52 / 4-37.

33. Readers of Bennett will recognize that I am opting for a reading of IIIP4 which he considers and rejects in §55.4. It seems to me that the reasons he gives for that reading are stronger than those he gives for rejecting it.

34. Matson raises this as a difficulty, though against a somewhat different formulation of the position, p. 407.

35. This is somewhat of a simplification. Cf. the letter to Elisabeth of January 1646: "When one considers the idea of the good which is to serve as a rule for our actions, one takes it for all the perfection which can be in the thing one calls good, and one compares it to the straight line, which is unique among the infinity of curves to which one compares the evils. It is in this sense that the philosophers usually say that *the good comes from the whole cause, the bad from some defect*. But when one considers the goods and evils which can be in one and the same thing, to know how highly to value it . . . one takes the good for everything which is found in it from which one can have some advantage, and one calls bad that from which one can have some disadvantage" (Alquié III, 635). This seems to me very close to the spirit of E IV Pref.

36. Allison (p. 235) suggests that Spinoza's interpretation of the *conatus* as involving a striving to increase one's power of action may have been inspired by Hobbes' argument that man's quest for power never ceases "because he cannot assure the power and means to live well, which he hath present, without the acquisition of more" (*Lev* I, xi).

37. Similarly, in EL I, vii, 1, Hobbes defines delight as an increase of vital motion, and pain as a decrease of vital motion. Cf. *Lev* vi, 10. It is tempting to see Hobbes' theory of vital motion as the ancestor of Spinoza's theory of the proportion of motion and rest. Cf. KV II Pref.

38. Cf. Bennett, §64.7.

39. I take it that this suggestion would not undermine the point I go on to make in the following paragraph, since the issue of calculation will arise only if the *conatus* doctrine is understood as being not merely a teleological principle, but what Bennett would call teleological-cognitive doctrine (§68.3), i.e., as having the form "if he thinks it would help him, he will do it."

40. For whom pity is "grief for the calamity of another . . . [which] ariseth from the imagination that the like calamity may befall himself" (*Lev* vi, 45). On this theme in Spinoza, see the meticulous analysis in Matheron, pp. 151ff.

41. Bennett (§64.7) contends that "Spinoza wants a doctrine of the emotional brotherhood of *all mankind*" and Matheron seems to imply something similar (p. 155). But however useful this might be for purposes of motivating an ethical egalitarianism, it seems to me to fly in the face of the facts, and I don't see that we are obliged to ascribe such a demand to Spinoza. The ethics of the free man at the end of Part IV (particularly PP70,71) seems to me to recognize that as things are there are morally significant differences between men, that the free man will properly behave quite differently towards other free men than he will towards the ignorant.

42. Cf. Matheron, p. 211. I think it would be fair to say of Hobbes that, although he recognizes in a way Descartes had not, the importance of laws of nature in a genuinely scientific human psychology (Cartesian psychology being primarily classificatory), he does not try to systematize these in the way Spinoza does.

43. In this section I draw heavily on my article, "Spinoza's Moral Philosophy," in the Grene anthology. For further detail see that article.

44. Bennett (§68.4) infers from the fact that there is no further discussion of the model that "this passage must be a relic of a time when Spinoza planned to make the concept of a favored model of mankind do some work for him in the body of Part 4." I would prefer to say that it is doing work in the body of Part IV, though that work may not be obvious. One thing it does is to provide a context within which IVD1,D2 take on a clearer and more specific meaning. The talk about models is not a defect which Spinoza should have repaired by elimination, but a guide to the interpretation of D1 and D2.

45. Ultimately, of course, it goes back to Plato's *Republic*, but the

evidence seems overwhelming that the immediate influence was Hobbes.

46. Cf. Nietzsche, *The Antichrist*, §7: "Christianity is called the religion of *pity*. Pity stands opposed to the tonic emotions which heighten our vitality. It has a depressing effect. We are deprived of strength when we feel pity. That loss of strength which suffering as such inflicts on life is still further increased and multiplied by pity. Pity makes suffering contagious" (Kaufmann, pp. 572-573).

47. Cf. *The Antichrist*, §24: "So that [the Judaeo-Christian morality] could say No to everything on earth that represents the ascending tendency of life, to that which has turned out well, to power, to beauty, to self-affirmation, the instinct of *ressentiment*, which here had become genius, had to invent *another* world, from whose point of view this affirmation of life appeared as evil, as the reprehensible as such" (Kaufmann, p. 593).

48. Cf. *The Antichrist*, §58: "One should read Lucretius to comprehend *what* Epicurus fought: not paganism, but 'Christianity,' by which I mean the corruption of souls by the concepts of guilt, punishment and immortality" (Kaufmann, p. 649). See also Nietzsche's comment on iiiP18s2 in his *Genealogy of Morals* ii, 15.

49. Cf. *The Antichrist*, §45: " 'For if you love them which love you, what reward have ye? do not even the publicans the same? And if ye salute your brethren only, what do ye more than others? do not even the publicans so?' (Matt. 5:46f). The principle of 'Christian love': in the end it wants to be *paid* well" (Kaufmann, p. 623).

50. Kaufmann, p. 92.

51. It seems to me that Bennett's criticism of Spinoza as a psychotherapist (in ch. 14 generally, but particularly in §76.2, par. 2, and §78.4, par. 3) is weakened by a failure to consistently acknowledge this point. Spinoza does give some excuse for thinking otherwise (e.g., in the wording of vP2, or in vP10s, ii / 289 / 10-12), but the passages in which he does so seem to me not to reflect his most considered view, which is better represented by vP4s, ii / 283 / 5-11).

52. There is an excellent account of this in Bennett, §63, though Neu's *Emotion, Thought and Therapy*, U of California Press, 1977, is also worth recommending. The tendency to incorporate a cognitive element in the definitions of the affects is also present in Hobbes, though to a lesser extent than in Spinoza. Cf. *Lev* vi.

53. Objection: "At the core of my hatred of W there is an unpleasant state of mind and a belief about W's causing something—but not

his causing my mental state! I could forgive that. What I will not forgive is the harm he caused to the American wilderness. I do think he caused my distress: I think he caused my beliefs about his actions, that those caused my unpleasure, and that causation is transitive; so, being rational, I think he caused the unpleasure. But that is because I have philosophical opinions about belief, emotion and cause; it is not at the heart of my hatred towards W" (Bennett, §63.6). Reply: "I think Spinoza might grant much of this, but deny that the case in question is a central case of hate. It's granted that W causes my displeasure, but insisted that he does this indirectly, by causing harm to the environment. This makes the case a particular species of hate, viz. indignation (i.e., hate toward someone who has done harm to another, DefAff20). But in simpler cases, the object of my hate may cause my displeasure directly. What must be common to all cases of hate, if Spinoza is right, is that directly or indirectly the object of hate is thought to cause displeasure to the one who hates him. Would it be correct to say that I hated W if I believed that he had harmed the environment, but did not believe that he had caused me any displeasure? No. Then my belief that he has caused me displeasure is as essential to my affect's being a case of hate as my belief that he has caused harm to the environment is to my affect's being a case of indignation." (Here and in the text I emend Spinoza's definition of indignation to: hate toward someone who *is believed to have done* evil to another.)

54. Cf. Bennett, §76.2. I've defended Spinoza's argument for this proposition at length in "Descartes, Spinoza, and the Ethics of Belief," in Mandelbaum and Freeman.

55. This is an empirical question, about which opinions may differ, but I was very surprised to see Bennett take the contrary view in §81.3, par. 3. There is an important school of psychotherapy which, so far as I can see, is based on the Spinozistic assumption I make in the text. See A. T. Beck, A. J. Rush, B. F. Shaw, and G. Emery, *Cognitive Therapy of Depression*, New York: Guilford Press, 1979.

56. The argument of this paragraph is suggested by, but distinct from, a criticism made by Bennett in §76.1. In spite of §63.5 I think it is an overgeneralization to suppose that all emotions must include a cognitive element, and that the cognitive element must always cause the non-cognitive element in the emotion.

57. See Bennett, §78.1.

58. Cf. Bennett, §78.1

INDEX OF PASSAGES DISCUSSED

GENERAL INDEX

LIBRARY OF CONGRESS CATALOGING-IN-PUBLICATION DATA

Curley, E. M. (Edwin M.), 1937-
Behind the geometrical method.

Bibliography: p.
Includes index.
1. Spinoza, Benedictus de, 1632-1677. Ethica. 2. Ethics—Early
works to 1800. I. Title.

B3974.C87 1988   170'.92'4   87-25850
ISBN 0-691-07322-8 (alk. paper)   ISBN 0-691-02037-X (pbk.)

Edwin Curley is Professor of Philosophy at the
University of Illinois at Chicago